A Labor of Love

COMPLIMENTS OF
Gwen Schwindt
Seniors Real Estate Specialist
Phone: (563) 349-1595 or Email
GwenSchwindt@RuhlHomes.com

"Grow old along with me!
The best is yet to be,
the last of life, for which
the first was made.
Our times are in His hand..."

– Robert Browning

A Labor of Love

My personal journey through the world of caregiving

Mary Schricker, SRES, CSA
Senior Real Estate Specialist
Certified Senior Advisor

A Labor of Love: My Personal Journey Through the World of Caregiving

Artwork and cover design by Bret Schricker, www.redboxdesign.org.

To the memory of my parents:
In living, you taught me the importance
of faith, hard work, integrity, and honesty.
In dying, you taught me about unconditional love
and the importance of family.

“In any project the important factor is your belief.
Without belief there can be no successful outcome.”

– William James

Life's Sunset: Acknowledgments

The writing and completion of this book was not a solitary voyage. It was the result of conversations with other professionals in the senior community, healthcare workers, co-workers, family, friends, and most importantly, caregivers who were also cast into this sudden role of life and death decisions. My thanks to all of you who took the time to share your stories. Some of your experiences were fodder for general information regarding caregiving and others were relayed in your own words for the reader to interpret and absorb. Special appreciation goes to Stephanie, Dick, Judy, Bill, Carolyn, Mary, Laurie, Mark, Gloria, Cheryl, and Patti for sharing your heartfelt words about your own personal tragedies and triumphs.

During my research, I found such topics as estate planning, financial preparedness, and funeral pre-arrangement pertinent to the caregiving process. Since these subjects are out of my area of expertise, I decided to turn to three well-respected professionals who agreed to compose articles for inclusion in the book. A special thanks to David Deuth, Jamieson Long, and Jim Tiedje for sharing this important information with my readers.

To my editor, Laurie Boyce-Steinhauser: Your talent and ability gives purpose and meaning to my otherwise unorganized thoughts and words. Your encouragement and friendship made all the difference during the ongoing process, and I thank you for that.

To my publisher, Terry Wilson: Thank you for your expert knowledge about the publishing industry, your honesty and wit, and most of all your friendship.

Thanks to the Graphic Arts Team at Moline Dispatch Publishing: You did an excellent job of reading my mind!

To my son, Bret: Thank you for using your artistic talent to contribute to the book. I know your grandma would be so proud that you added such depth to the meaning of my words.

To my son, Matt: Your gift of time to Grandma meant so much to her. No matter how busy, you always found time to run errands for her or to sit with her for long periods of time. You have no idea how much that meant to her and to me. Thank you for caring so very much.

To my sister, Brenda: This is your story too. Thank you for all of your help, physically as well as emotionally, throughout Mother's illness and during the months since her passing.

To my cousin Joan and family: Without your love and support through Grandma's illness, this project would never have reached fruition. Thanks for loving her and trusting my decisions.

To my friends: You are a constant source of support as well as a sounding board for my ideas and writing. You have honed your listening skills and never seemed to tire of my questions. Thanks to all of you for your friendship.

To the entire staff at Friendship Manor Continuing Care Facility: Words pale in my effort to thank you for all you did for my mother in her final months and days.

There is a vast amount of information regarding the topic of caregiving and only some of it has been touched on in this publication. My challenge in writing this project was to keep it informative and brief enough to read in one or two sittings. When faced with the challenge of caring for another human being, time is at a premium. I found in my research that, although many of the books I read contained much valuable information, it took a great deal of time to sift through the pages to find the basics. So this is a book of basics!

Hopefully, there is incentive and motive to research further if needed. It is also my wish that you have found a mirror of your own experiences somewhere in these pages. If you are not feeling so alone and have gleaned some insights to rely on during the remaining days of caring for your loved one, I have accomplished my goal. Best wishes to you in your journey. I hope you have a greater understanding of your mission and a greater appreciation for each and every day with which you are blessed.

Live long, live well, and live happy!

“Life isn’t about waiting for the storm to pass.
It’s about learning to dance in the rain.”

– Vivian Greene

Table of Contents

Something Has Happened: The "Ah-ha" Moments

xv Preface
1 Introduction
13 The Bad News Day
15 The Defining Moment
21 Anger, Fear, and Grief
29 Caring for a Spouse is Different

We Can't Pretend Anymore

39 Do Not Go it Alone
49 Choosing a Place to Live
65 What to Do With All that "Stuff"
69 Guilt
73 Just a "Little White Lie?"
75 The Importance of Humor

Afterthoughts...

81 Spirituality and Aging
87 The Cycle of Life
93 Anger, Fear, and Grief Revisited
99 End Epitaph

Helpful Material

103 Planning for the What Ifs, *by James R. Tiedje, CSA*
107 Advance Planning for Seniors, *by D. Jamieson Long, Jr., J.D.*
113 Remember Well, *by David Deuth, CFSP*
117 Bibliography
121 Additional Resources

Something Has Happened: The "Ah-ha" Moments

"Yesterday is not ours to recover,
but tomorrow is ours to win or lose."

– Lyndon B. Johnson

Preface

During the past few years as a Seniors' Specialist, I have had the opportunity to act as a sounding board for clients who have been thrust into the role of caregiver for a family member or friend. I have listened, mediated, and cautiously advised them. I have helped them liquidate assets, market and sell the family home, and often I have assisted them in finding appropriate placement for their parents and grandparents. It has been my professional persona; my contribution to preserving the dignity of our seniors. But never once did I really understand the magnitude of the emotional impact that those decisions had on the family members; not until the roles were reversed, and I was the advisee rather than the advisor.

With little warning, my mother had a stroke. Overnight I became a statistic… one of the 44.4 million Americans who are a caregiver. It was only then that I began to understand the pain and anguish that my clients had been experiencing. And as with any personal situation, the emotions clouded the facts.

I too was faced with problems like:

- What placement best suits my mom's physical and mental condition?

- What can she afford?
- What do I do with her condo — and a lifetime of possessions?
- How do I find time to run the errands, take her to the doctor, and visit her in the hospital while still working full-time?
- How do I deal with *my* anger at her for being so sick?
- And, lastly, but most importantly, how do I stay mentally, emotionally, and physically healthy through this stressful time?

After many sleepless nights, much needed vacation time, the support of friends and family, some soul searching, and the realization that I could not do it all alone, I worked through these problems and found reasonable solutions to most of them. I have emerged from this journey a more qualified professional, a stronger woman nourished by heightened spirituality, and a more enlightened caregiver who realizes that each healthy day we are given is truly the greatest of all gifts. I also hope that the adversity I have faced has made me a better mother, a more understanding sister, a loyal friend, and most importantly, a more loving and patient daughter.

If you are reading these pages you are possibly a caregiver to one of millions of people requiring assistance to get through the day. That loved one might be a spouse, a parent, a sibling, or a friend. Regardless of the relationship, 90% of the help he or she receives — help with shopping, bathing, eating, and medical care — comes from you.

Your job is exhausting, stressful, frustrating, and at times, completely overwhelming, but it is, without a doubt, a labor of love.

The journey on which you have embarked is an emotional roller coaster. Whether you have already had a long ride or just climbed on, my hope is that the following pages will offer some solace as well as some practical advice to guide you through the days of caring for your loved one.

The suggestions and information in these pages are addressed to a widely diverse population. Take what you will, use what applies, and do what feels right to you. No one answer can serve us all.

Somewhere out there is a unique place for you to help others — a unique life role for you to fill that only you can fill.

– Thomas Kinkade

“There are only four kinds of people in the world…

those who have been caregivers,
those who are currently caregivers,
those who will be caregivers,
and those who will need caregivers.”

– Rosalynn Carter

Introduction

We will probably all be caregivers to someone at some point in our lives. We may take care of a sick child, a friend who is recovering from surgery, or an aging family member. The levels of care we may provide are as diverse as the caregiving situation itself. In order to fully understand the pages to follow, it is necessary to define some terms and provide some general knowledge about caregiving and its effects on those involved.

Defining Caregiving

A caregiver is a person who assists another with his or her physical or emotional needs for a brief time or over an extended period of time. This help may be required for many of the activities or needs that healthy, active people take for granted and may include such things as:

- Walking;
- Bathing;
- Dressing;
- Using the bathroom;
- Incontinence;
- Managing pain;
- Preventing unsafe behavior (including wandering);

- Providing comfort and assurance;
- Providing physical or occupational therapy;
- Attending to medical needs;
- Counseling;
- Feeding/Eating;
- Answering the phone;
- Meeting doctors' appointments;
- Providing meals;
- Maintaining the household;
- Shopping and running errands;
- Providing transportation;
- Administering medications;
- Managing money (including paying bills);
- Doing the laundry;
- Attending to personal hygiene;
- Helping with personal grooming;
- Writing letters or notes;
- Making repairs to the home;
- Maintaining a yard;
- Removing snow.

Long-Term Care

The need for long-term care might be due to a terminal condition, disability, illness, injury, or simply old age. Estimates by experts are that at least 60% of all individuals will need extended help in one or more of the areas above during their lifetime. The need for long-term care may only last for a few weeks or months (temporary) or it may go on for years (ongoing). It all depends on the underlying reasons for needing care.

Temporary long-term care (need for care for only weeks or months) may include:

- Rehabilitation from a hospital stay;
- Recovery from illness;
- Recovery from injury;
- Recovery from surgery;
- Terminal medical condition.

Ongoing long-term care (need for care for many months or years) may include:

- Chronic medical conditions;
- Chronic severe pain;
- Permanent disabilities;
- Dementia;
- Ongoing need for help with activities of daily living;
- Need for supervision.

Ongoing long-term care services may be provided in any of the following settings:

- In the home of the recipient;
- In the home of a family member or friend of the recipient;
- At an adult day services location;
- In an assisted living facility;
- In a skilled care facility (nursing home);
- In a hospice facility.

The concept of caregiving or long-term care planning is fairly new. It has evolved gradually from these factors:

- Improved medical care and prevention efforts have contributed to dramatic increases in life expectancy. The growth in the number and proportion of *very* old adults is unprecedented in the history of our country. Concurrently, there has been a major shift in the leading causes of death from infectious diseases and acute illnesses to chronic diseases and degenerative illnesses.

- There has been a trend toward smaller and more diverse families. Since 1970, the percentage of households containing five or more people has fallen by half. Meanwhile, the "Ozzie and Harriet" family model has given way to a collection of diverse family structures: single parents, blended families, cohabiting couples, and two-wage earner families.
- The number of "dispersed families" has dramatically increased. It is no longer unusual for adult children to be living in a geographically different location than their parents.

LOL :)

Three retirees, each with a hearing loss, were taking a walk one fine March day.

One remarked to the other, "Windy, ain't it?"

"No," the second man replied. "It's Thursday."

And the third man chimed in, "So am I. Let's have a Coke."

Who Receives Care

From the American Association for Retired Persons (AARP) and the National Alliance on Caregiving:

- Most care recipients are female (65%) and many are widowed (42%).
- Nearly eight out of ten care recipients are age fifty or older.
- The average age of all care recipients over fifty is seventy-five years-old.
- Caregivers who provide for someone fifty or older tend to be helping their mothers (34%), grandmothers (11%), or fathers (10%). Sixty-five percent of these caregivers say other unpaid caregivers assist them in their role. Forty-six percent said they also employed paid help within the past year.

- The primary problem for most care recipients is simply "aging," followed by diabetes, cancer, and heart disease.
- One quarter of caregivers for those fifty or older report the person they care for is suffering from Alzheimer's, dementia, or other mental confusion, but only 8% say it is their main illness.
- More than half of care recipients (55%) live in their own homes.
- More than nine out of ten (92%) care recipients fifty or older take prescription medicine.

Caregiver Stress

While there are deep rewards, caregivers are exposed to a wide range of stressors, including strains on the emotional, physical, and financial aspects of their lives. According to AARP and the National Alliance on Caregiving:

- Three factors have the greatest effect on the caregivers' emotional stress, physical strain, and financial hardship due to caregiving. They are: the level of burden, whether caregivers feel they had a choice in the decision to become caregivers, and caregivers' reported health status.
- More than half (57%) of working caregivers say they had to go to work late, leave early, or take time off to provide care.
- Women contribute more hours of care, provide higher levels of care, and feel they have less of a choice in assuming the caregiving role than men. These factors increase women's risk for

emotional stress and a diminished quality of life.

- Of those providing more intense levels of caregiving, 84% say they have less time for friends and family; 76% report less time for vacations, hobbies, and social activities; and 49% say they are getting less exercise than before becoming a caregiver. Thirty-four percent of those caregivers who provide more intense levels of care say it has made their health worse.
- Additionally, an estimated 40% of the caregivers in the United States are middle-aged men or older and it appears these men are rolling up their sleeves, jumping in, and getting their hands dirty. Whether caring for an elderly parent or an ill spouse, more and more men are in it for the long-haul, committing themselves to always "be there" for their loved one. For generations, women have typically been the caregivers for any family members in need. This was often due to men being the primary "bread winners" and women being home and more available.

The employee-caregiver problem is a relatively new phenomenon. A fast-growing generation of elderly people needing care is starting to put a great deal of pressure on both employed caregivers as well as employers. Caring for an older family member has become a way of life for millions of working Americans who are trying to balance employment and the responsibilities of caregiving. Nearly half of the caregivers are employed full-time, with an additional 11% employed part-time. Not surprisingly, employed caregivers, with their emotions in overdrive, are often exhausted, burdened, and stressed. As increasing numbers of baby boomers continue to age, this employee-caregiver problem, dubbed the "silent productivity killer," will continue to grow.

Geographic distance can add another dimension to the already challenging role of caregiver. While someone else might provide the primary, day-to-day attention, approximately seven million Americans are long-distance caregivers for aging adults who live an hour or more away. These caregivers must juggle the demands of two households while pre-arranging schedules, business meetings, and doctor appointments. If you are a long-distance caregiver, consider the following suggestions:

- Make sure they know how to reach someone in an emergency. Seek out help from people in the community: the next door neighbor, an old friend, the doctor. Call them. Tell them what is going on. Make sure they know how to reach you.
- Take steps to identify options to help the primary caregiver. He or she may not need the help now, but having plans and arrangements in place can make things easier if there is a crisis.
- Find a directory of senior services by checking with a library or senior center for lists of resources. Get several copies — one for yourself and one for the primary caregiver. This helps everyone

learn what is out there and perhaps to start "plugging into the networks." Don't forget to check for updates.

- Pull together a list of prescriptions and over-the-counter medications. Get doses and schedules. This information is essential in a medical emergency. Update it regularly.
- During a visit, go through the house looking for possible hazards (such as loose rugs, poor lighting, unsafe clutter) and safety concerns (such as grab bars needed in the bathroom). Stay for a weekend or a week and help make needed improvements.
- Find out if there is an advance directive stating healthcare treatment preferences. Copies should be distributed to the primary caregiver and physician for future reference. If not, talk about setting one up.

Another option available to long-distance caregivers is the use of a Geriatric Care Manager (GCM). A GCM is a professional specializing in the needs assessment and arrangement of services for older people. They are usually nurses, social workers, or gerontologists. The GCM can:

- Make an initial assessment of care needs;
- Suggest options for meeting identified needs;
- Provide referrals to local resources; and
- Arrange for services to be implemented.

There are many additional resources from the U.S. National Institutes of Health and the National Institute of Aging. You can access information at www.niapublications.org. One example of an excellent resource available is "So Far Away: Twenty Questions for Long-Distance Caregivers." This timely and handy guide offers answers to the following inquiries:

1. What is long-distance caregiving?
2. How will I know if help is needed?
3. What can I really do from far away?
4. How can my family decide who does what?
5. Are there things I can do that will help me feel less frustrated?
6. What is a Geriatric Care Manager and how can I find one?
7. How can I keep up with my mom's medical and health care?
8. How can I make the most of a visit with my parent's doctor?
9. How on earth can my parents afford everything they need?
10. What kinds of documents do we need?
11. Should I encourage my parents to get more help?
12. How can we make the house safer for my mother who has Alzheimer's disease?
13. How can I lighten the load for my mother?
14. How can I help my folks decide if it's time for them to move?
15. What happens if my mother gets too sick to stay at home?

16. How is it that long-distance caregiving makes me feel so guilty all the time?
17. How can I be sure my father's caregiver isn't mistreating him?
18. How can I help my parents think about their future health care preferences?
19. What is the difference between an advance directive and a living will?
20. What if I'm told my mom only has a few months to live?

The following are additional security tips to ensure your loved one's home is safe. For more suggestions, contact www.howtocare.com/home.htm.

To improve lighting and visibility:

- Place light switches close to room entrances;
- Install light switches at the top and bottom of the stairs;
- Use high-watt light bulbs in stairways and other hazardous areas;
- Provide sufficient, even lighting throughout the home;
- Install additional lighting if necessary;
- Install a voice- or sound-activated adapter to turn on lights and appliances;
- Install under-the-cabinet lights in the kitchen;
- Place a night light in the path between the bedroom and bathroom;
- Install cordless battery-operated lights inside closets and cabinets;
- Install motion-sensitive exterior lighting.

To enhance safety and support:

- Remove loose rugs;
- Secure mats with non-skid backing or double-sided carpet tape;
- Secure telephone and electrical cords;
- Install non-slip flooring especially in the kitchen and bathrooms;
- Use non-skid mats or adhesive strips in the bathroom;
- Remove thresholds;
- Rearrange furniture to move it out of paths and walkways;

- Place barriers at dangerous locations;
- Edge stairs with bright, non-skid tape to highlight changes in floor levels;
- Install rubber treads on uncarpeted indoor and outdoor stairs;
- Install handrails and grab bars, particularly in stairways and bathrooms;
- Clamp adjustable safety rail onto edge of bathtub;
- Install anti-scald devices on faucets and shower heads;
- Install smoke detectors near the kitchen and bathrooms;
- Install plug-in carbon monoxide detectors;
- Install a portable security intercom;
- Install an emergency response system.

To improve accessibility, ease of use, and convenience:

- Install a wheelchair ramp;
- Arrange furniture to leave wide corridors for wheelchairs and walkers;
- Ensure chairs have arms and seats that are high enough to allow for easy sitting down/getting up;
- Widen doorways by removing moldings and replacing hinges;
- Install revolving shelves;
- Convert a ground-floor room into a bedroom;
- Install a bedrail and/or handrails;
- Install a commode (portable toilet) in the bedroom;
- Lower closet shelving and cabinets;
- Install slide-out shelving, adjustable rods, baskets, and other closet organizers;
- Replace round doorknobs with lever handles;
- Attach lever adapters to round doorknobs;
- Install lever-handle faucets in kitchen and bathrooms;
- Replace fixed shower heads with flexible hand-held shower heads;
- Install a raised toilet seat;
- Install a shower or tub chair;
- Install crank-operated windows;
- Buy clocks with large numerals;
- Buy telephones with large buttons.

LOL :)

This 85-year-old couple, having been married almost 60 years, had died in a car crash. They had been in good health the last ten years, mainly due to her interest in health food and exercise.

When they reached the pearly gates, St. Peter took them to their mansion which was decked out with a beautiful kitchen and master bath suite and Jacuzzi. As they "oohed" and "aahhed," the old man asked Peter how much all this was going to cost.

"It's free," Peter replied. "This is heaven."

Next they went out back to survey the championship golf course that the home backed up to. They would have golfing privileges every day and each week the course changed to a new one representing the great golf courses on earth.

The old man asked, "What are the green fees?"

Peter's reply, "This is heaven. You play for free."

Next they went to the club house and saw the lavish buffet lunch with the cuisines of the world laid out.

"How much to eat?" asked the old man.

"Don't you understand yet? This is heaven. It is free!" Peter replied with some exasperation.

"Well, where are the low-fat and low-cholesterol tables?" the old man asked timidly.

Peter lectured, "That's the best part... you can eat as much as you like of whatever you like and you never get fat and you never get sick. This is heaven."

With that, the old man went into a fit of anger, throwing down his hat and stomping on it, and shrieking wildly. Peter and the old man's wife both tried to calm him down, asking him what was wrong.

The old man looked at his wife and said, "This is all your fault. If it weren't for your blasted bran muffins, I could have been here ten years ago!"

The Bad News Day

My journey began in February 2007, while on my way home from a vacation. A neighbor of my mother called and reported that she had taken my mom to the emergency room with a migraine headache. I assumed that my mom would be given medication, released, and life would continue as it had. Little did I know that this was the beginning of the end of my mother's healthy, independent lifestyle. The years since that eventful night were marked by deteriorating health, a loss of independence, and a mourning for a life and relationship that once existed. I watched my vibrant, eighty-five year-old mother, a lady in the truest sense of the word, age overnight. Our Sunday morning breakfasts after church, our all-day shopping trips, my mother's home cooked meals, and life with Grandma as the matriarch all ended in a twenty-four hour period. It took all of us, her family and friends, much longer to realize the loss.

Not everyone's news comes as decisively as mine did. Sometimes it manifests itself in the form of a nagging pain, a slight loss of memory, or the wear and tear of years of age. Others experience a heart weakened by attack after attack, a stroke magnified by continuous TIAs (also called "mini-strokes"), a devastating cancer diagnosis, or a gradual diminishing of physical and mental capacities. Regardless of the cause, the end result is often a loss of ability to function on a day-to-day basis independently without some assistance from others. That is when our job begins. And that is when the questions and concerns begin creeping into our subconscious, and we come to the realization that our loved one cannot make it alone. That is when we climb onto the roller coaster; **our ride has begun!**

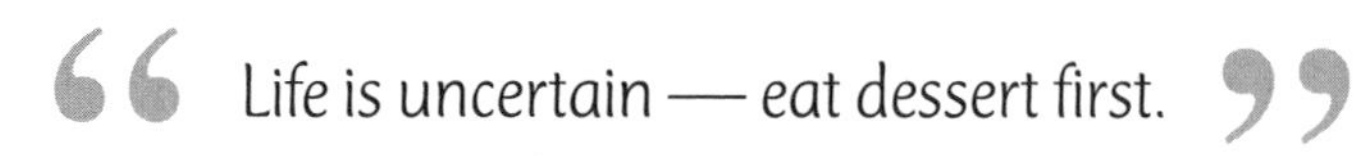

The Defining Moment

During the years of parenting my two sons, I often thought about and followed the advice inherent in the quote by Hodding Carter: "There are two lasting bequests we can give our children: One is roots; the other is wings."

Children are brought into the world and cared for by their parents until they are able to fend for themselves. Many parents would probably agree that it is difficult to let go and admit that their children are independent enough to handle life's decisions and challenges. The "wings" part is often much more difficult than the "roots." So it is naturally a bit unsettling for parents when the tables are turned and the children are now in the position of taking care of them.

When a parent grows frail over a period of time or a sudden illness leaves him or her dependent, roles shift uncomfortably. It is a delicate balance between helping and advising parents and protecting them from the dangers that might be brought on by their deteriorating physical or mental condition. Giving up independence is not something anyone wants to do. Maintaining the familiarity of our lives becomes paramount to our everyday living. In today's culture, we are generally conditioned to hide our aging and not accept it as natural and inevitable. Loss of independence is difficult to hide and becomes an embarrassing condition instead of an ordinary part of the continuum of life.

As people age, they are protective of the lifestyle for which they have worked so hard. They surmise that they should be able to live where they want and come and go when they please. Unfortunately for some, that is not possible — at least to the extent they wish.

Adding to this difficult situation is the fact that parent-child conflicts, which may have been swept under the rug for years, begin to resurface. Many of us spent a better part of our lives fighting our parents for own independence and identity and now we wish with all our heart we did not have to be in charge.

The Sandwich Generation

When I was in the throngs of raising my children as a single parent, I remember getting a call from my mother telling me that my dad's health was declining; his already weak kidneys were failing, and he would have to go on dialysis. Anyone who has experienced this regimen knows that it is physically and emotionally draining both on the patient and the caregiver.

I was already overloaded with the responsibilities of having two teenage sons and two full-time jobs, but like many of my generation, I felt I owed it to my parents to be there for them as they struggled through this crisis. Little did I know that I was a classic example of the "Sandwich Generation," those people locked between caring for their own children and caring for their aging parents. Holding a job and raising a family in today's world is hard enough without having to worry about college, retirement, and concerns about elderly parents. But this is just what many baby-boomers are faced with since 75% of their parents are likely to need some kind of physical or financial help at the very time when their own children are making the greatest demands on their time and resources. Research indicates that as many as one out of eight Americans, ages 40 to 60, is raising a child *and* caring for a parent at home. Additionally, seven to ten million Americans are caring for their aging parents from a long distance away.

When my dad's health started to fail, my parents lived in St. Louis, more than 270 miles away from me. One of the challenges I faced in dealing with my mom and dad was my tendency to want to completely control my parents' decisions.

I spent my days in the classroom where I had to make sure that everyone was amenable and under control. My second job as a realtor required careful scrutiny of contracts and compliance of rules and regulations. Then I went home to two teenagers where consistency in routines and rules was paramount. I spent the better part of my days and evenings making sure I was in control of every situation presented to me, so as you may expect, it was difficult to be patient with my parents' situation, which consisted largely of the unknown.

Without thinking, I wanted to just bulldoze ahead and tell them what they *should* be doing without regard to their frustration, confusion, and fears. I had to remind myself that they needed to be handled in a way that would preserve their dignity. My dad's health crisis would change dramatically how they dealt with every aspect of their lives. My own sadness about my dad's physical deterioration added more emotional anxiety to an already overstressed environment.

During the entirety of my dad's declining condition, my mother was in remarkable health for a woman her age. She was committed to catering to my dad's every need, and it was not until after his death that I realized what impact the intense caregiving had on my mom. Although she was still free from any major medical problems, she had become frail and weakened from the continued stress.

As I came to terms with my parents' scenario, I realized that due to the physical distance separating us, my function had to be that of an emotional caregiver. I decided a meaningful role I could play was that of intermediary between the medical personnel and my parents. Translating the difficult medical jargon and procedures into laymen's terms and explaining available options eased some of the stress for my dad. I talked with them often and visited whenever I could. It was important to me that they knew I was there for them but not trying to control their lives.

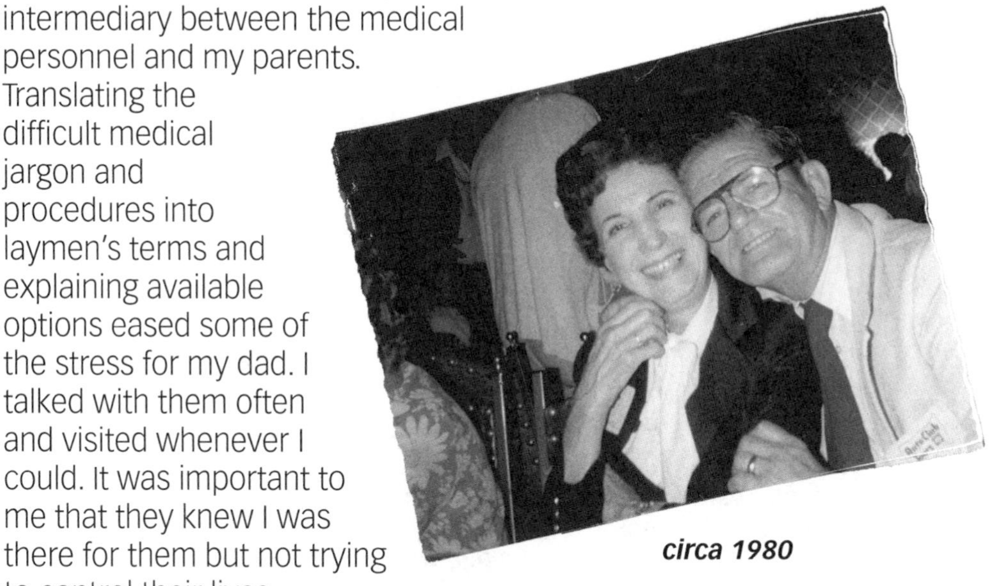

circa 1980

The term "Sandwich Generation" was coined and defined by Carol Abaya, a nationally recognized expert on aging and elder/parent care issues. As a result of caring for her own parents and talking with caregivers around the world, she categorized the different scenarios involved in being a part of the Sandwich Generation:

- Traditional: Those sandwiched between their own children and their aging parents who need care and/or help.
- Club Sandwich: Those in their 50s and 60s sandwiched between aging parents, adult children, and grandchildren, or those in their 30s and 40s with young children, aging parents, and older grandparents.
- Open Face: Anyone else involved in elder care.

In an age of extended life spans, increased medical technology, delayed childbirth, and transient lifestyles, the numbers of families sandwiched between generations will only increase. In twenty-five years, there will be sixty million Americans between the ages of 66 and 84, many of them needing full- or part-time care at the very time their grandchildren will be making the greatest demands on their parents' time. This crisis in caregiving has only just begun.

LOL :)

An old man visits his doctor and after a thorough examination, the doctor tells him, "I have good news and bad news. What would you like to hear first?"

Patient: "Well, give me the bad news first."

Doctor: "You have cancer. I estimate that you have about two years left."

Patient: "OH, NO! That's awful. In two years my life will be over! What kind of good news could you probably tell me, after this?"

Doctor: "You also have Alzheimer's. In about three months, you are going to forget everything I told you!"

Anger, Fear, and Grief

There is no blueprint for caring for our loved ones. It is not a role any of us audition for; so when we get the part unexpectedly, we are completely unprepared. During the years of being a caregiver to my mother, my emotions tended to be at a heightened state.

Anger came first for me. About fifteen years before my mother's stroke, I had been thrust into the role of a divorced, custodial mother of two sons, ten and twelve years-old. It was one of those life changing events that had certainly knocked the wind out of my sails. The lessons that I learned during the rebounding years left me a stronger, more self-sufficient, and less vulnerable woman. When my sons took flight as successful young adults on their own, I came to the realization that "now" it was my turn. My successful professional persona allowed me a sense of autonomy to live my life with few encumbrances. My comfortable freedom came to an abrupt end the day my mother had her stroke.

Millions of us travel down this road. Two or three decades have been spent raising our children, and now caring for a dependent parent or spouse looms on the horizon. Not exactly how we planned on spending our retirement years! Rationally we know that no one becomes old, or frail, or ill on purpose, but harsh words and rash actions can be symptoms of our irrational behaviors. In addition to the anger from our own selfishness, there is often a knee jerk reaction to the anger that the ill person is experiencing. After I realized I would be caring for my mom on a more permanent basis, I began to feel suffocated, and all I could think of was, "How could she do this to me?"

circa 1945

Through most of her life, my mom maintained an even keel of emotions. Her southern Georgia upbringing had taught her to keep her feelings at bay. After her stroke, however, she was not always able to do this. Her feelings of helplessness and loss of independence often manifested itself in yelling matches with me. I knew before the words flew out of my mouth that my reaction was inappropriate and certainly not conducive to helping her make peace with her newfound situation. I discovered after a time that when the anger welled up, it was best to remove myself from the setting, either by ending the phone conversation or exiting quickly with a promise to return at another time.

After many months of watching my mother's health deteriorate, I realized that much of what I was feeling was fueled by fear. Imminent in my mind was the fear that my mother was not going to get better, the fear that she was probably going to die sooner rather than later, and finally the fear that this entire scene might replay itself twenty or thirty years down the road with me as the victim.

It took me a long time to recognize the fears that my mother was facing. I since have surmised that she was probably afraid that her pain would become more intense, that she would end up alone and forgotten, and that she would be a burden physically and financially on her family. Most of all I think that, although she may not have feared death itself, she was afraid of the process of dying. I did not do a very good job of talking with her about her fears, but I did have a greater understanding of what she was going through, which tempered my anger and turned it into compassion. I also came to terms with my mother dying long before it actually happened.

The Beginning of My Grief

Grief is defined as a normal reaction to the feeling of loss. I learned that grief has many layers. Long before her physical death, I had already begun to mourn the loss of my mother in everyday activities which I had shared with her. I missed joining her in church on Sunday morning and going out to breakfast following. Holidays were not the same as they had been. She couldn't make my favorite cookies or the fruit cake I so loved. My sons also missed Grandma's cooking. Due to medical and physical restrictions, she could not travel. Shopping for special gifts for loved ones was no longer possible, and she was unable to attend the frequent lunches with her lady friends to celebrate a birthday.

One day I was sitting quietly in my mother's room at her care facility watching her struggle with walking just a few steps, and I realized that I hardly recognized this woman. I have thought about that moment many times since; it was then that I came to the realization that the mother I had known, the one with whom I had shared so many significant times in my life, was already gone. That was the second part of my grief. I cried most of the way home that day from her room. Other types of grief have followed, ultimately culminating in the day of my mother's actual physical death. Odd as it may sound, for me, that day was one of celebration, for her suffering had finally ended, and God called her to a greater and more peaceful place.

We all grieve differently and it is important to remember that it is a normal reaction to the loss of both the relationship we had and the actual person we knew. Our feelings during our grief process have no specific order. Anger, depression, and bargaining may come and go again and again while we struggle with the acceptance that our loved one is not coming back. There is no right or wrong way to grieve and we must all do what works for us as individuals.

 No one ever told me that grief felt so like fear. 

– C.S. Lewis

A CAREGIVER'S REFLECTION...

Watching my mom lie there in the end was one of the hardest things for me. She was the mother of our family, taking care of everyone, never forgetting birthdays or anniversaries...

~Judy

Grief differs greatly from person to person and is not an easy thing to "categorize." However, there are some signs that normal grief has moved beyond healthy mourning. A bereavement coordinator, trained therapist, or professional counselor can be of significant help and guidance if you feel your grief is atypical. The following information comes from http://www.helpguide.org/mental/grief_loss.htm.

When Grief Doesn't Go Away

It's normal to feel sad, numb, or angry following a loss. But as time passes, these emotions should become less intense as you accept the loss and start to move forward. If you aren't feeling better over time, or your grief is getting much worse, it may be a sign that your grief has developed into a more serious problem, such as complicated grief or major depression.

The sadness of losing someone you love never goes away completely, but it shouldn't remain center stage. If the pain of the loss is so constant and severe that it keeps you from resuming your life, you may be suffering from a condition known as complicated grief. Complicated grief is like being stuck in an intense state of mourning. You may have trouble accepting the death long after it has occurred or be so preoccupied with the person who died that it disrupts your daily routine and undermines your other relationships.

Symptoms of complicated grief include:

- Intense longing and yearning for the deceased;
- Intrusive thoughts or images of your loved one;
- Denial of the death or a sense of disbelief;
- Imagining that your loved one is alive;
- Searching for the person in familiar places;
- Avoiding things that remind you of your loved one;
- Extreme anger or bitterness over the loss;
- Feeling that life is empty or meaningless.

Distinguishing between grief and clinical depression isn't always easy, since they share many symptoms. However, there are ways to tell the difference. Remember, grief is a roller coaster. It involves a wide variety of emotions and a mix of good and bad days. Even when you're in the middle of the grieving process, you will have moments of pleasure or happiness. With depression on the other hand, the feelings of emptiness and despair are constant.

Other symptoms that suggest depression, not just grief:

- Intense, pervasive sense of guilt;
- Thoughts of suicide or a preoccupation with dying;
- Feelings of hopelessness or worthlessness;
- Slow speech and body movements;
- Inability to function at work, home, and/or school;
- Seeing or hearing things that aren't there;
- Feeling like life isn't worth living;
- Wishing you had died with your loved one;
- Blaming yourself for the loss or for failing to prevent it;
- Feeling numb and disconnected from others for a long time;
- Having difficulty trusting others since your loss.

If you recognize any of the above symptoms of complicated grief or clinical depression, talk to a mental health professional. Left untreated, complicated grief and depression can lead to significant emotional damage, life-threatening health problems, and even suicide. But treatment can help you get better.

A CAREGIVER'S REFLECTION...

I cannot believe how many of our friends' parents we have lost this past year; I know five friends who are mourning their loss. It's also a reminder that we are beginning to sit on the top of the heap — inevitable though it may be, it is still unreal to me to believe that we are getting older. Turning 40 or 50 is nothing compared with losing the generation ahead of us.

My husband has really listened to me a lot these past few months. He has lived a long time without his mom and almost five years without his dad now. Not that it is easier for him — although he says it **is** *more "normal" now. He likened the loss to a room you visit. You go into the room a lot when your loved one first dies and then, ever so slowly, you don't go into the room as often. But the room is always there; sometimes you peer in, but you don't go all the way in. He said it will not be as powerful or as strong a missing as I feel now. I have to say that I am grateful for having been close to Mom. I didn't always understand our relationship, but I was comfortable and happy with her.*

~ Laurie

circa 1944

Caring for a Spouse is Different

As my parents entered their retirement years, they decided to winter in Florida. By the fall of 2000, my dad's health had deteriorated such that travel was difficult for both him and my aging mom. Since I had just become an "empty-nester" and had not yet launched my full-time real estate career, I offered to come to Florida and help out. During those months I saw for the first time the immense job my mother had as my dad's caregiver. Due to kidney failure, my dad was on dialysis, resulting in every-other day visits to the dialysis center. His diabetes and heart condition required that my mother prepare special meals. He tired easily, and although he enjoyed the sunshine and

bottom photo circa 1992

warm weather, he was still relegated to spending much time indoors resting. During the many years my mom took care of my father, she never complained. Her actions were born out of the love and belief in the words "in sickness and in health," that she had spoken over sixty years before.

Caregiving for a spouse is a much more complex journey than caring for one's parent. I recognized that although my focus was on taking care of my parents, many people my age were also faced with caring for spouses who had become ill or disabled. As I listened to the people who had experienced spousal caregiving first-hand, I realized that although there certainly was some common ground, the reactionary differences were immense. How we respond to the illness and death of a parent is so very different than how we deal with the same issues with regard to a spouse. Parental aging, although painful, is a natural occurrence of the cycle of life. The loss of a spouse is unnatural and unnerving.

As I conversed with others, another topic emerged: the differences in how men and women handled the caregiving process. It seemed from my research that being the caregiver was more difficult for men. Male caregivers are more likely to hold their emotions inside, creating more stress by not opening up and talking about their feelings. Often, men refrain from asking for help until it is far too late.

I spoke with several men about their experience of caregiving for their wives. Some common factors emerged from these insightful interviews.

- Men are less likely to be able to take off work. It is often more acceptable for a woman worker to take time off or take a leave of absence to be a caregiver. My interviewees felt a man, asking for the same thing, might be refused the request.
- Many of these men felt a sense of guilt that they had not done enough to help their wives during their illnesses.
- Many felt they had not done a very good job of truly caring and being empathetic to their wives. Some felt that they were just innately incapable of caregiving as well as women.
- Most of the men felt overwhelmed by the additional jobs with which they were faced: laundry, cooking, cleaning, and in some instances, child care.
- One man said his wife had always been his rock, the one he turned to when he was having a down day. She would make him laugh and realize that everything was going to be okay. When his wife was no longer able to do that, he felt lost and had nowhere to turn.
- One of my sources suggested that there is a need for a "grief recovery model" for men, run by men, with no women present. I found that men had fewer opportunities to vent both during their wives' illnesses and after their death. Support programs are language-driven, and many men are not comfortable sitting in a circle "exposing" themselves to others emotionally.

In interviewing women who were caregiving for their spouses, I found there was much more acceptance of their duty or role. They just seemed to know what needed to be done, and in reality, there was little time for guilt or regret. They accepted that, although life wasn't exactly what Cinderella would have chosen, it was the hand they had been dealt. They did feel a bit overwhelmed with some of the physical demands of caring for their loved ones as well as the house and yard. They all admitted that they had become more resilient, both emotionally and physically, as a result of their experience.

There is no doubt that men and women approach caregiving differently just as they do with most challenges presented to them in life. It is not to say that one is better than the other. Much of it has to do with the tools we are given, what we are comfortable with, and the roles society expects of us to play.

A CAREGIVER'S REFLECTION...

My dad hired a cleaning lady when my mom was dying. He had a strong sense of guilt for having always thought her job as a "stay-at-home mom" was not really a job.

- Cheryl

A New Chapter

The death of a spouse is tragic at any point in life, but losses that occur after forty, fifty years of marriage or longer can be devastating. One loses not only the individual, but the daily routine, the companionship, valued social roles, and what some describe as "a large piece of themselves." Some bereaved spouses feel that the world as they knew it vanished. Loss of a loved one and being unable to do anything about it is very disempowering. Grieving individuals may feel they no longer have control over anything, including their own emotional response to the loss. There are ways to regain that control and begin a changed but new life. The following are several useful suggestions to help with the grieving process.

- Allow yourself to mourn. Mourning is an open expression of thoughts and feelings regarding your loss. Mourning the death of a loved one is essential to be able to heal.
- Take life one day at a time. Grieve at your own pace. Do not compare yourself to others and do not expect your grieving process to follow a set time frame.
- Talk to friends and family about the death of your loved one and how this makes you feel. Talk about your life with your loved one. Share your memories — those that make you laugh and those that make you cry.
- Forgive yourself for any emotions that you might feel while trying to cope with the death of your loved.
- Go easy on yourself. You might be tired. You may be unable to make decisions. All of this is a normal part of coping with the death and will pass in time.
- Listen to your body. Be sure to take care of your own physical needs.

- Deal with your loved one's belongings only when you are ready.
- Give yourself permission to heal. It is important to remember that healing does not mean forgetting. Enjoying life again does not mean that you do not miss your loved one. When you find yourself beginning to heal, allow it to happen.
- It is normal for some people to feel guilty when experiencing a new relationship but moving beyond your grief does not mean you will forget your loved one. You will always carry that person within your heart as you go forward. And do not be surprised if grief resurfaces from time to time. There will be moments when grief may appear temporarily for the rest of your life. *This is normal and healthy.*
- Starting to date again is an important part of the healing process and can be very rewarding, yet it takes courage. When you are ready to date again, celebrate your courage and the new possibilities as you begin this new chapter in your life. It can happen again!

A CAREGIVER'S REFLECTION...

I find that [my husband] David's birthday, holidays, etc., have all become easier to handle because I changed my behaviors, Christmas traditions, and such. Most of all, I am able to tell people I actually don't feel differently on these special days, because I miss him every day. I might recall more fond memories which are the ones I choose to remember, but I do not feel sad.

~ Carolyn

Elizabeth Levang, Ph.D., in her book, *When Men Grieve*, states:

"To say that men are unable to describe their emotions is not to say that men lack feelings. Men as a whole have not created a language of grief for themselves. Men have been raised mute, silent to their emotional pain. In our culture, men are expected to be in control, in all situations and at all times, whether at home, work, or in a social environment. Men must not show weaknesses of any kind, or be overly dependent on others for support, advice, or encouragement. They are encouraged to be dominant, aggressive, powerful, and capable. If men don't have the answer, they're supposed to know where and how to find it. Men approach life believing that there isn't a problem that can't be solved. For many men, grief is just another problem to solve — just another of life's challenges, another test of manhood."

We Can't Pretend Anymore

circa 1955

circa 1950

Do Not Go it Alone

In almost every family there is one person who takes charge in times of crises. Whether it is the result of birth order, geographical proximity, avocation, or simply character make up, this one person assumes the primary responsibility of caring for the family member in need. Regardless of your personal situation, the stress of caregiving can leave lasting effects on the dynamics of the family. In any given year, there are more than forty-four million Americans who provide unpaid care for an elderly or disabled person over the age of eighteen. Informal caregivers provide 80% of the long-term care in the United States. The typical caregiver is a forty-six year-old woman with at least some college who provides more than twenty hours of care a week.

Caregivers are more likely to have symptoms of depression and anxiety. Due to time constraints, they are less likely to eat healthily or get enough sleep and physical activity. They often ignore routine diagnostic procedures to stave off serious health problems.

Just a few months after my mom lost my dad, she made the decision to move to Iowa to be closer to my sister and me. With her living in a condo down the street from me, I became a minimal caregiver for my mother, watching over her well-being and sharing an occasional social or family activity. When she became seriously ill, it made perfect sense that I be the one in charge. Since I had networked extensively on a professional level in the senior community, I knew who to contact to answer the many questions I had about my mother's care and placement following her stroke. My sister would come to help often, but geographic distance as well as job demands limited the help she could provide. And, quite frankly, I am not sure I asked…at least not until the stress and demands of taking care of my mother began to affect my mental and physical well-being. The daily visits to the hospital and subsequently to the nursing home were taking a toll both on my personal life as well as my health.

Some of the best advice I received came from my general practitioner. He and I both understood that the stress of caregiving was causing me some health issues that, if not attended to, could become much more serious. He suggested that I restrict my visits to a few times a week, and ask others to run errands or transport my mother to doctor appointments. My mother, who was experiencing considerable anger over her situation, would often call me with complaints several times a day. It was suggested that I designate a special phone ring for her, calling her back at my convenience, hopefully after she had worked through some of her anger. That was one of the best pieces of advice I received.

The responsibility for my mom's care weighed heavily on me. There were times I resented my sister (and maybe everyone else) for not being able to help more with the day-to-day duties. There were many nights when I awoke disturbed by the thoughts that maybe I was not doing everything I could for my mom. I would vacillate between my doubts and the frustration that it was all on my shoulders. When I talked with others about their family dynamics, I realized I was pretty fortunate. My sister, although not always able to be physically present, was 100% supportive of every major decision made with regard to my mother's health care, dispersing of the property, and facility placement. My two sons, who lived close by, were my "Rocks of Gibraltar," and often my sounding board for decisions.

I am not naïve enough to think that every family can work things out as well as my sister and I did. I realize I am one of the lucky ones, for to have to deal with family discord on top of all of the other problems can be even more taxing and insurmountable. Some of the practical solutions I gleaned from my own personal experience may help your family members and you better manage this difficult time.

- Ask for and accept help.
- Learn to say "No."
- Don't feel guilty if you are not the "perfect" caregiver. Just do your best.

- Identify what you can and cannot change. You cannot change someone else's behavior, but you can change how you react to it.
- Set realistic goals. Break larger tasks into smaller steps for both the person for whom you care and you.
- Prioritize, make lists, and establish a routine.
- Find out about caregiving resources in your community.
- Make time for yourself.
- Eat healthily and get exercise and as much sleep as time allows.
- See your doctor for routine checkups.
- Keep your sense of humor.

I often see, in my professional capacity, families who cannot agree on anything. The demands of caregiving often bring out old behavior patterns and unresolved tensions. Past wounds are re-opened and childhood rivalries re-emerge. How we handle situations in life is based on our habits of communication marked by various degrees of aggressiveness, passiveness, or assertiveness. Our habits are a result of the influences from both our small and large cultures.

Our small culture is best defined as our immediate family and the people with whom we have spent our life. Our habits of communication can be altered as our small culture changes throughout our life; however, the people closest to us continue to leave an impression on our communication habits.

The larger culture that influences us is our nationality or heritage. Not all nationalities handle life's challenges in the same way. In patriarchal cultures, the women have little or no say in the decision-making process. Some cultures forbid anyone from the outside to care for their aging family members. Other cultures are guided by religious beliefs that govern decisions regarding medical treatments. The assumption by individuals that everyone involved in the decision-making process perceives and interprets information the same way may lead to disruption and alienation of family members. Add to the already tense situation large doses of guilt and anxiety, and you have a potentially explosive scenario. So how do you move forward? It is recommended that an outside person be brought in to facilitate communication and find common ground. This facilitator can be a professional mediator, minister, legal advisor, Geriatric Care Manager, or a close friend.

Of those caregivers caring for someone who is over fifty years of age:

- 67% are women;
- 33% men;
- 59% are married;
- 23% are high school graduates;
- 26% are college graduates.

A CAREGIVER'S REFLECTION...

The summer my mom died, I lived three hours away. I had just had my fourth child, and my husband had a series of unexpected surgeries. I was frustrated that I had so little time to spend with my mom. I was also upset: one of my sisters felt I should not help make any decisions about Mom's care because I wasn't there every day. Another sister understood my predicament and included me in on choices and conversations. She listened to my concerns about Mom. I wanted to support my siblings' decisions, but I wanted my opinion to matter also. To this day, I am grateful for my sister's perception and inclusion.

- Laurie

The Family and Medical Leave Act

Ask your human resource office about the Family and Medical Leave Act. You may be able to take up to twelve weeks (unpaid) vacation for caregiving responsibilities.

The Family and Medical Leave Act (FMLA) is a federal law that lets covered employees take extended time away from work to handle certain family or medical needs. Many states have similar laws that may provide additional coverage above and beyond that outlined in the FMLA.

Not every employer is required to provide its employees with family or medical leave. Federal law states that an employer is required to provide eligible employees with leave if the employer is either:

- A state, local, or federal governmental agency, or
- A private business engaged in, or affecting, interstate commerce that employed fifty or more employees in twenty or more weeks in the current or prior calendar year.

This criteria may sound complicated, but in reality, virtually every business in the U.S. engages in, or affects, interstate commerce. The "fifty or more employees" standard includes everyone on the employer's payroll, including part-time employees, employees on approved leave, and leased or temporary employees.

An employee who works for a covered employer is eligible for leave if he or she worked for the employer for at least twelve months, or for at least 1,250 hours over the twelve months immediately preceding the need for leave. The employee must also work at a worksite in the U.S., or a U.S. territory, at which the employer has at least fifty employees within seventy-five miles.

What leave is provided?

The requirements set out here are those under the federal FMLA. Laws in individual states may have other requirements that provide leave to more (or different) employees.

A covered employer must provide eligible employees with a maximum of twelve weeks of leave. That leave may be unpaid, but it may be combined with accrued paid leave (such as vacation or sick leave). An eligible employee may take leave:

› For the birth, adoption, or placement of a child;
› To care for a spouse, minor or incompetent child, or parent who has a "serious health condition," or
› To handle the employee's own serious health condition that makes him or her unable to work.

A "serious health condition" is defined as an illness, injury, impairment, or condition that involves:

› Hospital care;
› Absence from work, plus continuing treatment;
› Pregnancy;
› Treatment for a chronic condition;
› Permanent long-term supervision; or
› Multiple treatments.

Employees may be required to provide advance notice, if possible, and medical certification of the need for leave. An employer who provides health insurance is required to maintain coverage for an employee on leave on the same terms as if the employee had continued to work.

When an employee returns from leave granted by the FMLA, he or she is entitled to be restored to his or her former job, or to an equivalent job, with equivalent pay, benefits, and other terms of employment. Taking leave may not result in the loss of any benefit to which an employee was entitled before taking leave, and may not be counted against an employee under a "no-fault" attendance policy.

Certain employees may be denied restoration of their jobs if returning them to their former positions would result in substantial and grievous economic harm to the employer. A "key" employee is defined as a salaried employee who is among the highest paid ten percent of the employees within a seventy-five mile radius. An employer must notify an employee that he or she is a key employee when the employee gives notice of intent to take leave, and must notify the employee when a decision is made to deny reinstatement.

Elder Abuse Facts from the National Council on Aging

Elder abuse refers to intentional or neglectful acts by a caregiver or "trusted" individual that lead to, or may lead to, harm of a vulnerable elder. Types of abuse include physical, sexual, financial or material exploitation, abandonment, neglect, and emotional or psychological.

Key Facts

- *How many elders are abused?* According to the Department of Justice, a minimum of one in nine or 11% of Americans over age 60 have experienced some form of elder abuse in the past year.
- *Many cases go unreported.* For every one case of elder abuse, neglect, exploitation, or self-neglect reported to authorities, at least five more go unreported.
- *Who commits elder abuse?* In almost 90% of the elder abuse and neglect incidents with a known perpetrator, the perpetrator is a family member, and two-thirds of the perpetrators are adult children or spouses.
- *Financial abuse is common.* Elder financial abuse is regarded as the third most commonly substantiated type of elder abuse, following neglect and emotional/psychological abuse. While underreported, the annual financial loss by victims of elder financial abuse is estimated to be at least $2.6 billion.
- *Reports increasing.* As the number of elders increases, so does the problem. Adult Protective Services (APS) found that elder abuse reports have increased by 16% comparing data from 2000 with that of 2004.
- *Death rates higher.* For those elders who have been mistreated, the risk of death is 300 times greater than those who have not been.
- *Women and the very elderly are most at risk.* Elder abuse affects seniors across all socio-economic groups, cultures, and races. However, women and "older" elders are more likely to be victimized. In 2003, two out of every three (65.7%) elder abuse victims were women, and in twenty of the states, more than two in five victims (42.8%) were age 80 or older.

The National Center on Elder Abuse advises that if you suspect an elder is in a dangerous or life-threatening situation, call 911 immediately. If you suspect elder abuse and want to report it or get more information, you can call 1-800-677-1116 to find the Elder Abuse Help Lines and Hotlines for your state.

When you call to report elder abuse, be prepared to provide the following information:

- Your name and contact number, but if you prefer to remain anonymous, you can still report elder abuse.
- The elder's name, address, and contact number.
- What types of support the elder has (including family, doctor, or other medical workers, friends, and healthcare workers who could be helpful).
- Details about why you suspect elder abuse or are concerned about the possibility of elder abuse, including physical evidence (bruises, burns), hitting, yelling, poor nutrition, or other threats to the elder.

Keep in mind that you don't have to prove that elder abuse is taking place — that's the job of the investigators. If you have even the slightest suspicion that someone is the victim of elder abuse, talk to someone about it.

LOL :)

Three ladies were discussing the travails of getting old. One said, "Sometimes I catch myself with a jar of mayonnaise in my hand, standing in front of the refrigerator, and I can't remember whether I need to put it away or start making a sandwich."

The second lady chimed in, "Yes, sometimes I find myself on the landing of the stairs and can't remember whether I was on my way up or on my way down."

The third one responded, "Well, ladies, I'm glad I don't have that problem. Knock on wood," as she rapped her knuckles on the table, and then said, "That must be the door. I'll get it."

Choosing a Place to Live

I remember the day so very clearly. It was the day I had to tell my mother that she would not be returning to her condo; that, due to the magnitude of her stroke, she could no longer live alone. It was one of the most difficult things I have ever had to do. Over the past few years I have advised hundreds of families on this same matter, but somehow when it came to my own mom, I was at a loss for words.

When people grow old, the decision about where to live is one of the most important choices they can make. The quality of their housing and neighborhood and the communities in which they live influence whether they have satisfying and rewarding lifestyles. To make this choice against their will and without honoring their input is so very difficult. No one wants to "place" their parents or spouse in a facility with strangers, but the fact is a majority of seniors will not live out their lives in their own house. If someone had asked me a few years ago if I would have admitted my mom to a nursing home, I would have emphatically said no. I had planned to have my parents live with me if they became disabled and could not manage on their own.

What I had not counted on was that my mom would require twenty-four hour medical assistance, which I could not personally nor financially provide. Sometimes if our loved ones require constant attention by licensed medical professionals, we have no choice but to admit them to a facility that can provide that necessary level of care. For my mom this meant moving from her 1,400 square foot condo to a very small room shared with a stranger in a facility where the average occupant was in much worse mental shape than my mother.

We held onto my mom's condo for a few months hoping for the miracle that would allow her to return home. Once we realized that she was too weak to ever live alone, my sister and I decided to begin the process of selling her condo and liquidating its contents. We had my mom come to the house one last time to sort through some of her belongings and try to decide what she would have room for at the nursing home. In reality, it would have taken days and days for her to go through all of her belongings. We made the decision to do most of it without her, since the emotional pain of having to dispose of a lifetime of belongings was too much for my mother in her frail condition. She was very angry that we did this, and it was many months before she forgave us. Regardless of her reaction and our subsequent guilt, I still feel under the circumstances, we made the only choice we could to provide her with the care she needed, free from harm.

The decision about where to place my mom was relatively easy for our family since the choices of facilities were limited due to her specific physical condition. She had been placed on a feeding tube which required around-the-clock medical assistance; therefore, independent and assisted living facilities would not accept her. We chose a continuing care facility since it offered a full continuum of housing and services within the same community.

Fortunately, the range of housing options available for the seniors of today is growing rapidly. Traditional nursing homes as we have known them only represent a small end of the growing spectrum of choices. The first step in finding the right kind of in-home care is determining what level of care is needed. There are two main levels of care: skilled and custodial. Skilled care provides for medical needs and custodial care deals with environmental and personal needs such as housekeeping, shopping, bathing, dressing, etc. Ask neighbors, friends, medical workers, and caregivers for referrals. There are also numerous federal, state, and local agencies specializing in senior/aging care that can give you names of reputable in-home care companies in your area.

Selecting Housing

Searching for and choosing appropriate placement for your loved one is an arduous and time consuming task. Do not be afraid to ask for help from both friends and experts you might know in the healthcare field. Here are several suggestions that might help if you are faced with making a residency choice.

- Word of mouth recommendations are an excellent place to start. The opinion of someone you know and trust is the most reliable source you can have.
- Contact the social service specialist at your local senior center to access a list of available facilities.
- Religious social service organizations may also be helpful.
- Your family doctor, hospital social worker, or Geriatric Care Manager can provide you with good leads and general information about the type of facility your loved one might need.
- Organizations such as the Alzheimer's Association, Parkinson's Association, or the National Stroke Association will provide you with a list of facilities that might be equipped to meet a specific type or level of care.
- Your local Area Agency on Aging can provide you with a list of licensed care facilities in your community.
- The Internet is a useful tool especially if you are a long-distance care provider.

The following is a brief description of the types of senior housing available in most areas:

Accessory Apartments, also known as in-law apartments or "granny flats," are viable options for relatively healthy, independent seniors who are comforted by being close to loved ones. This option offers proximity and added security while preserving privacy. It can be a costly choice if major renovations need to be completed.

Senior Apartments are housing units set up specifically for elderly residents. They provide privacy and independence while offering limited services such as meals, housekeeping, laundry, and transportation. These are often government subsidized and sometimes have long waiting lists.

Assisted Living Facilities are best suited for individuals with physical or cognitive impairments that make it difficult for them to perform an average of two activities of daily living (ADLs) without assistance. ADLs include six basic personal care activities: eating, toileting, dressing, bathing, transferring, and continence. Assisted living facilities offer those services plus meals, housekeeping, and planned social and recreational activities. What distinguishes this type of facility from other types of congregate living is the on-site staff is available twenty-four hours, seven days a week for protective oversight to meet both the scheduled and unscheduled needs of the residents.

Skilled Care Facilities, also known as *Nursing Homes,* provide shelter and care for disabled individuals or seniors who have more serious health problems, functional impairments, or cognitive deficits, and who often require twenty-four hour skilled nursing care. On average these residents need help with more than three ADLs. Residents admitted to these care facilities typically have multiple health problems. Most offer around-the-clock nursing supervision and on-call physicians in addition to meals, laundry services, personal care, counseling, recreation, nutritional guidance, social services, rehabilitative programs, and pharmacy and laboratory services. While skilled care facilities are typically needed for long-term care, they are also used for brief periods of recuperation after hospitalization for patients who plan on returning home.

Continuing Care Retirement Communities (CCRC) offer the full spectrum of care, from apartments to assisted living unit's to skilled care facilities. These are a popular choice with families due to the peace of mind knowing that future care is covered, and additional "placement" decisions will be minimal. These communities are designed with the "aging in place" theory. A person can move in while still an active member of society and remain there for the rest of his or her life, moving into other parts of the facility as one's health dictates. These facilities offer the full menu of services and health care as needed. People can choose a CCRC at any stage of physical or cognitive need depending on available space and funds.

In-Home Health Care: Most seniors would prefer to remain in their homes as long as it is possible. In many instances, the aging person may not need constant medical attention, but cannot function independently without some assistance. In this scenario, in-home care might be a viable option. As we age, it becomes more difficult to perform tasks that are a part of our normal daily activities. These instrumental ADLs include light housekeeping, buying groceries, preparing meals, opening and sorting mail, paying bills and balancing bank accounts, shopping for necessities such as clothing and prescriptions, and even planning and participating in social activities. Other ADLs such as bathing, brushing teeth, shaving, and dressing become a challenge as we age and our bodies become less cooperative. Aging people who do not have spouses or companions or other family members to whom they can turn for assistance should consider hiring in-home care providers to help them so they are not uprooted from their homes before it is absolutely necessary. The presence of an additional care provider can also greatly reduce the burden placed on family members who are emotionally and physically stressed by the added responsibility of caring for an ill or aging spouse or parent.

In-home care is the most commonly asked for service among today's aging population. In-home care involves a network of service providers who deliver personal care and maintenance right in the home, so an individual is able to continue living independently in familiar surroundings. In many cases, the in-home care provider also gives the aging or ill individual companionship during the long days or evenings. It certainly can give the other family members peace of mind while they are at work or attending to the other responsibilities of their own children and spouse.

A CAREGIVER'S REFLECTION...

My mother had a strong and negative emotional reaction to hospice. She wasn't ready to die and hospice symbolized the reality of her impending death. The care she needed wasn't possible in a hospital setting. Hospice not only took care of her medical and personal needs, but they cared for our comfort and emotional needs as well, which allowed us to focus our attention on supporting her and each other. I was able to be with her as she died — holding her in my arms and talking to her — letting her know that my father and I would be okay and she could leave.

- Cheryl

Hospice

Choosing a setting for your loved one's remaining days can also be contingent on the extent and type of care needed to ensure the best quality of life. If your loved one has been diagnosed with an incurable or progressive illness and has a limited life expectancy, hospice might be something the family wants to consider. Hospice care can be provided in an independent setting, an assisted living facility, a skilled care facility, in one's own home, or in a hospital.

Hospice is a concept of caring that has its roots in medieval times when it symbolized a place where travelers, pilgrims, and the sick, wounded, or dying could find rest and comfort. The hospice movement in the United States began with the work of British physician Dame Cicely Saunders and Swiss-born psychiatrist Dr. Elisabeth Kübler-Ross who brought the subject of death and dying into the open. The first hospice house in America, the Connecticut Hospice, opened in 1974. In 1978, the U.S. Department of Health, Education, and Welfare published a report citing hospice as a viable concept for terminally ill people and their families that provides humane care at a reduced cost. Today, there are more than 3,200 hospices across the country. According to the National Hospice and Palliative Care Organization, in 2000, about one in every four Americans who died received hospice care at the end of his or her life...roughly 600,000 people.

Hospice offers comprehensive healthcare services for people with a terminal illness. It emphasizes comfort care rather than curative treatment. Hospice is described as holistic: it looks and addresses the patient's physical, emotional, and spiritual well-being and offers supportive services for all family members and loved ones.

Hospice includes medical care with an emphasis on pain management and symptom relief. Hospice care takes place wherever the need exists. It can be at a hospital or special hospice center, but 80 % of hospice care takes place in the patient's home. Hospices serve people of all ages who are coping with end-stages of chronic diseases and offer state-of-the-art palliative care, using advanced technologies to prevent or alleviate distressing symptoms. Hospices rely on the combined knowledge and skills of an interdisciplinary team of professionals to coordinate an individualized plan to care for each patient and family. Hospices employ physicians, nurses, home care aides, social workers, chaplains, therapists, bereavement coordinators, and counselors. As a family-centered concept of care, hospice focuses as much on the grieving family as on the dying patient. The gift of hospice is its capacity to help families see how much can be shared at the end of life through personal and spiritual connections.

LOL :)

A reporter was interviewing a 104-year-old woman. "And what do you think is the best thing about being 104?" the reporter asked.

She simply replied, "No peer pressure."

Palliative care means more than just treating the symptoms. It now often refers to a comprehensive approach to improving the quality of life for people who are living with potentially fatal diseases while also providing support for family members. In a palliative care program, a multidisciplinary healthcare team works with both the patient (with a possibly fatal illness) and family to provide medical, social, and emotional support. The team might be made up of doctors, nurses, therapists, counselors, social workers, and spiritual advisors. Palliative care is not just for those who might die soon, but is a resource for anyone with a long-term illness. It can be provided at home, in a hospital, nursing home or skilled care facility, out-patient clinic, or other specialized setting.

A CAREGIVER'S REFLECTION...

In the spring of 2005, I returned home to be with my mother for her surgery for breast cancer. When I arrived, my mom seemed a little tense. Her oncologist had called that day and told her they found a spot on both her liver and her lung during her pre-op. We went for a three-mile walk, and I remember being in a fog, mostly from the tears, but also from not really knowing what would happen next.

Typical of my mom, she insisted that we just take things one day at a time. Through the entire journey, I found that my mom faced her death the same way she faced her life: with dignity and determination. As an only child with my father's death looming in my past, I faced each day exactly how my mom asked me to. She was determined for me to work until she said it was "time." When it was time, she said we would know.

One early morning in August as I ended a run, I thanked God for the many blessings he had given me and for the beautiful day that was before me. I also asked, "God, if you are going to take my mom, would you please bring someone tall, dark, and handsome to take care of me?" A couple of weeks went by and my mom was feeling pretty well. I was in a routine of running, working, and coaching. Out of the blue, Sean entered my life.

Then my mom's condition began to change. The call came. It was time. Sean came with me when I went home. He had never met my mom, and he really did not know what was ahead of us. The next ten days I faced my mom's death how she expected: with strength and courage. We cried, we laughed, we hugged, and we were just there together. Her sense of humor about the end was incredible. We needed to make a decision to move her to a bigger room to accommodate more visitors; but the bigger room did not have a bathroom. She told me to do whatever I thought was best. I said that space was needed more than the bathroom since she couldn't use it. She looked at me and said, "Wishful thinking, I guess."

I remember holding her hand and telling her, "Mom, I will be okay. It is time for you to be with Dad." (She had never remarried and hardly dated since my father died.) When she slipped into a coma late in the afternoon of October 8th, she squeezed my hand and said, "Steph, I love you."

Two days later I walked into the hospice house; she looked like an angel. I told her I loved her. At ten minutes past 10:00, on the tenth day she had been in hospice, Mom died. Looking back, this was the most peaceful thing I had ever experienced.

The pastor at Mom's funeral reminded us that there were three things Mom didn't want: a church funeral, a picture in the paper, and tears for her. At the beginning of the service, the pastor said, "We know that Sondra has joined her soul mate, Ron, as they look down on us from the veranda in heaven having a cocktail."

She was the "Wind Beneath My Wings," the song I performed at her funeral.

~ Stephanie

627·751
ED & MARGE

Las Vegas
13

Gander
MOUNTAIN

What to Do With All that "Stuff"

Our society often defines a person by the quality or quantity of his or her possessions. We spend our lives buying, collecting, and accumulating. It's no wonder as we age our attics and basements are filled with treasures, and we are faced with the ominous task of sorting and tossing out years of memories.

For some, this is a pre-planned trip down memory lane; family members choose and take items with special significance to them. But all too often the necessity of "de-cluttering" is born of grief for a lost loved one or a lifestyle that has vanished.

A good definition of clutter might be a possession that does not *enhance* one's life on a regular basis. This, of course, varies with each person as our interests dictate what we might accumulate as well as what we value. For instance, for an avid reader, an entire room full of books would not be clutter. Clutter goes far beyond things in our physical environment.

Complicating the downsizing process is all the emotional baggage attached to a person's valuables. This is especially true of older people since the sentimental ties to the accumulated items can be very intense. Identities are often connected to our possessions. Unloading them feels like giving away a part of ourselves. Those who have endured a time when they had to "make do" with very little have a much more difficult time throwing anything away. We are the sum of our experiences and many of our seniors have lived through harder times and frugality, which has often led to shelves and drawers full of plastic tubs and glass jars, twisty-ties and sugar packets, as well as used aluminum foil and washed-out plastic bags. Often, the mindset for many older people is, "I better not throw it away, because I might need it for something someday."

It may also be increasingly difficult for someone who has lost a loved one to de-clutter since those possessions may be filling a hole in his or her heart. If you are faced with the task of downsizing or helping a loved one sort through his or her belongings, you might find the following suggestions helpful:

- Start in the storage area or least-used rooms.
- Concentrate on one room at a time.
- Begin with six large boxes.
- Label each box or section of the room according to the following categories:
    - › Items you will give to family or friends;
    - › Items you will donate to charity;
    - › Items you will keep;
    - › Items you will sell;
    - › Undecided;
    - › Garbage.

Keep the first step of sorting simple. If you get caught up in who will get Grandma's china early on, you will not feel you are accomplishing much.

As you sort, ask yourself the following questions:

- Does the item have sentimental value?
- Does the item take up much needed space?
- When was the last time the item was used?
- Does this item serve a purpose now or is it just being kept because it used to be needed?

As you dig through the belongings, you will run across items and pictures that will bring back memories. Allow time to savor those reflections and to mourn the losses that occurred. You may find that this takes longer than expected and that it is an emotionally and physically exhausting job.

Our needs change as we age: this is as natural as cycles and seasons of the year. Passing on treasured items and the traditions that often surround them is a way of giving each of us a little bit of immortality. It is a gift to friends and family — one that can extend to those who have never met you, as well as to future generations.

A CAREGIVER'S REFLECTION...

I kept my mother's robe and wore it like a hug when I missed her. I encouraged my own kids to take a sweater or shirt of their father's for the times they would miss him.

- Cheryl

LOL :)

"How was your golf game, Dear?" asked Jack's wife.

"Well I was hitting pretty well, but my eyesight's gotten so bad I couldn't see where the ball went."

"Well, you're 75 years-old now, Jack. Why don't you take my brother Scott along?" suggested his wife.

"But he's 85 and doesn't even play golf anymore," protested Jack.

"But he's got perfect eyesight. He could watch your ball," his wife pointed out.

The next day, Jack teed off with Scott looking on. Jack swung, and the ball disappeared down the middle of the fairway. "Do you see it?" asked Jack.

"Yup," Scott answered.

"Well, where is it?" yelled Jack, peering off into the distance.

"I forgot."

Guilt

It would be far easier for me to list the things I do feel guilty about than those I do not. I am a member of the generation that was raised on guilt. I am not sure if I ever really remember being punished too severely as a child because my parents "guilted" me into doing the right thing most of the time. Guilt is an emotional warning sign that we learn through our normal childhood social development. Its purpose is to let us know we have done something wrong, to help us develop a better sense of our behavior and how it affects ourselves and others. It prompts us to re-examine our actions so that we do not end up making the same mistake again.

During my mom's illness, my guilt could be summed up as follows:

- When I was with my mother, I felt guilty that the other responsibilities at home and the office were being neglected.
- When I was at home or at the office, I felt guilty that I was not spending enough time with my mom.

I know that my guilt stemmed from my inability, no matter what I did, to make matters right again…to restore my mother to her relatively healthy pre-stroke existence. As caregivers we are set up for failure from the beginning, for no matter what we do we cannot save or rescue our loved ones. We become helpless in the face of the inevitable, and somehow we get caught up in thinking we are responsible for the life or death of that person. In reality, we can only be responsible for keeping him or her comfortable for as long as possible.

Guilt is destructive. It slows the normal grief process since it drains much needed energy. The guilt I experienced during the two- and one-half years of my mother's struggles was one of the most difficult things for me to work through. Toward the end of my mother's illness, I felt completely consumed by my role as her caregiver. I woke up one day and realized that I needed to separate myself for a while from the caregiving role. The stress was causing me to have some health problems. It was difficult to concentrate on tasks at hand, both personally and professionally. More importantly, I was beginning to resent my mother for her unintended intrusion into my otherwise tidy life. That realization led to my decision to leave town for a few weeks and to ask my sister to take over until I returned.

My mother was angry at me for leaving, her friends did not understand my actions, and I am not sure at the time, my own family was very accepting either. In my absence, my mother was hospitalized several times. My sister, who lived ninety miles away, took time off of work and spent many hours and days by my mom's bedside. Relatives traveled from St. Louis to see my mom, and my sons made more frequent visits to Grandma. My decision to get away had a fortuitous and remarkable effect. The result was that everyone else, not just me, spent some quality time with my mother during her final days. My sister later thanked me for leaving, for during this time she was able to come to terms with my mother's dying…and say her good-byes.

That time away allowed me to return rested, healthier, and at peace with the knowledge that I had done all I could for my mother. When Mom died six weeks later, we were all so much more prepared. The recollections we had from those final months served as a bond that allowed family and friends to share the happy memories we had of my mom's life.

bottom photo circa 1996

LOL :)

A man asked his wife, "What would you most like for your birthday?"

She said, "I'd love to be ten again."

On the morning of her birthday, he got her up bright and early and off they went to a theme park. He put her on every ride in the park: the Death Slide, the Screaming Loop, the Wall of Fear. Everything there was, she had a go.

She staggered out of the theme park five hours later, her head reeling and her stomach upside down. Into McDonald's they went where she was given a Double Big Mac with extra French fries and a strawberry shake. Then off to a movie theatre, more burgers, popcorn, cola, and sweets. At last she staggered home with her husband and collapsed into bed.

Her husband leaned over and asked, "Well, Dear, what was it like being ten again?"

One eye opened, and she groaned, "Actually, I meant dress size."

Just a "Little White Lie?"

As my mom aged and the effects of her stroke limited her physical and mental capabilities, I struggled with helping her find a balance in that change. During the first few months of her ordeal, she was unable to drive. At that time, none of us knew how permanent her situation was, but we were pretty sure that at the age of eighty-eight, her driving days were over. After several failed attempts to convince her that she would no longer need her car, we dropped the subject. Whenever she would ask about her car, we would tell her it was in the garage. *What we failed to mention was that it was in the garage of the person to whom we had sold the car.* That was when I realized that lying by omission might be necessary. I did feel guilty about not being totally truthful, for I had never really lied to my parents (except for maybe a couple of times when I was a teenager…). I did conclude that the total truth at this stage of my mother's life might be too much for her to handle.

My mom's ability to swallow had been affected by her stroke, thus requiring that all nourishment be taken through a feeding tube. The doctors were relatively sure that her condition was irreversible, but to tell her that truth would have vanished all hope that she might one day again enjoy her favorite foods. Instead, we often talked with her about what she thought she might eat when she regained her ability to swallow food.

From the day my mom was admitted to her care facility, she was sure it was only temporary. We even had a hard time getting her to unpack her belongings, but after a while we convinced her she should put things away so she could find them. She relented but continued to declare that she would be going home soon. At first I was determined to make her see that returning to her condo was not a safe alternative. I now understand that convincing her would have eased my guilt about what I had done. After many unsuccessful attempts, we decided to just agree with her when she talked about returning home. We found ourselves saying, "Maybe tomorrow," or, "We'll have to see what the doctor says," or, "You work on getting stronger and we'll see!"

I am not saying that the end justifies the means. In our situation, the emotional impact that the truth had on my mother might have been worse than allowing her to believe that she could return to some semblance of independence again. It is often difficult to find the balance between honoring the patient's right to be involved in the decision-making process and shielding him or her from the truth that could quell any hope one might have of recovering. It is a tightrope that every caregiver walks. I found a melding of intellect and emotion with a heavy dose of empathy worked best for me.

The Importance of Humor

"Laughter is the shortest distance between two people."

–Victor Borge

Several months after my mom's first stroke, I agreed to take her shopping. She had lost a considerable amount of weight and needed new clothes. My mother was shuffling very slowly through the store aisle. In my impatience, I suggested to her that she pick up her feet and walk a bit faster… I commented that she looked like an old lady when she shuffled. She replied, "I am an old lady." Without thinking I said, "Well, you don't have to act like one." We looked at each other and both burst into laughter. I learned in that moment that it was okay to find humor in an otherwise bleak situation.

In later weeks and months, it was not unusual for my sister or me to walk into my mother's room and find that she had put her clothes on wrong-side out or that the buttons on her blouse were not lined up. Our immediate response was to take over and redress her; after awhile we learned to laugh first and then find a gentle way to remedy the situation. My mother complained daily that the phone did not work; again our initial reaction was to tell her the phone worked fine when it was hung up properly. Approaching the situation with humor allowed us to find ways to tease her about losing her phone without putting her on the defense. There were many more times during the ensuing months before her death when we chose laughter over confrontation and tears.

I am not suggesting that the situation you are dealing with is "any laughing matter." But approaching it with an aura of doom and gloom does not help anyone feel better. No matter how sick your loved one is, nor how incompetent you might feel, it is okay to laugh. In fact, the worse things get, the more important it is to find something about which to laugh. Your emotional core needs strength, and laughter will recharge it. There are many things in life over which we have no control. As long as we have a sense of humor, we can minimize the hold those upsetting situations might have on us. Humor helps us cope. Remember that laughter is an affirmation of our humanness; a way to express our anxieties, fears, and other hidden emotions. It breaks the ice, builds trust, and draws us together into a common state of well-being.

UCLA's Jonsson Cancer Center began a five-year study in 2000 to see if laughter improved pain and immune function with children suffering from cancer and other types of chronic diseases. The study showed that children had decreased levels of pain when they watched funny videos.

Many other studies demonstrated that laughter had many other positive results including:

- Decreased blood pressure;
- Increased oxygen utilization;
- Increased endorphin levels resulting in a greater sense of well being;
- Decreased cortisol levels resulting in decreased levels of stress;
- Promoted relaxation;
- Decreased depression;
- Improved immune function;
- Improved lung function.

Laughter allows us to fully express our emotions and feelings in a positive way. A robust laugh, often referred to as "inner jogging," gives the muscles of your face, shoulders, diaphragm, and abdomen a good workout. Laughter and humor are two powerful tools that can help people get through difficult situations. They are a source of power, healing, and survival. Noted comedian Bill Cosby once stated, "If you can find humor in anything, you can survive it!"

Humor is emotional chaos remembered in tranquility.

– James Thurber

> The term "humor" derives from the humoured medicine of the ancient Greeks which states that a mix of fluids known as humours, controlled human health and emotions. An imbalance among the humours resulted in pain and disease. Now centuries later medical studies are finding that a good healthy laugh can reduce stress, lower blood pressure, elevate our mood, boost the immune system, and improve brain functioning.

Afterthoughts…

LOL :)

Little Johnny and his family were having Sunday dinner at his grandmother's house. Everyone was seated around the table as the food was being served.

When Johnny received his plate, he started eating right away.

"Johnny, wait until we say our prayer."

"I don't have to," the boy replied.

"Of course you do," his mother insisted. "We say a prayer before eating at our house."

"That's at our house," Johnny explained. "But this is Grandma's house, and she knows how to cook."

Spirituality and Aging

While attending service at the Fort Myers Beach United Methodist Church, I listened to a choir member tell the congregation, made up largely of snowbirds, that his summer had presented him with some medical challenges but all had ended well. Bill Venzke then said, "If God brings you to it, he will bring you through it."

I have thought a lot about how powerful these words are. Our belief that God does help see us through difficult situations is one reason why houses of worship across America are often full of aging individuals.

From *Working with Seniors: Health, Finances, and Social Issues,* Susan H. McFadden writes…

"Look around most congregations at worship and witness the courage and persistence of the aged men and women who arrive with walkers and oxygen tanks, often transported by other older people less encumbered by health problems. Sharing pews with noisy babies, children with crayons, bored teens, and distracted parents, they sing and pray, sit in silence, listen to scripture and sermons, rise and sit as they are able, share the Eucharist if Christian, and exit in friendly conversation with fellow travelers. In the hymns, prayers, scripture readings, and sermons, they hear of love and forgiveness, gratitude and hope, despair and lamentation, anger, fear, and awe. In no other community do persons of so many different backgrounds and ages meet regularly to consider the human condition and turn to the sacred for an enduring sense of meaning and purpose in life."

Spirituality and religion can play an important role in the lives of many seniors. The later years of life are often a time for spiritual introspection. In fact aging is often referred to as a spiritual journey.

I grew up in a Christian home guided by Christian values. Through my life I have relied heavily on my faith to get me through both my every day existence and the larger challenges presented to me. In later years when my mother moved nearby, she and I would often attend church followed by the traditional Sunday morning breakfast outings. My mother, a product of a "Bible Belt" southern church, was perceived to be a woman of great faith. And although I know in my heart she believed, I saw her faith waiver during her final days. She seemed to blame God for what was happening to her. I tried to talk to her about it, but I could not get her to attend church service at the nursing home chapel. The minister from our home church was a frequent visitor, and I do know his words and prayers comforted her in her final days. My mother's anger at God may have simply been her inability to control what was happening to her.

People of any age who become ill or disabled need to make sense of the situation. In my mother's search to understand she was simply asking, "Why is this happening to me?" Our faith and spirituality and to what extent we rely on it is a very personal thing. Each of us has to find how it can best serve us during difficult times. As a caregiver it is important to remember that faith may ease your burden as you bear witness to, be present at, and give expression to your loved one's journey toward the end of his or her life. On this journey you may also be able to help your loved one search for the meaning of life, and most important of all, to help find hope that extends beyond the grave. I like to think that I was able, in some way, to help my mom better understand this in her final days.

> "Before you go to bed give all your cares and troubles to God.
> He's going to be up all night anyway."
>
> – Anonymous

CAREGIVERS' REFLECTION...

The last three or four days before Mom died we stayed with her 24/7, even sleeping in her pajamas at night. One morning we had all gone to church to celebrate Mass when the hospice nurse called and said the end was near. It was a gloomy day, but when Mom died, the sun came out; the sunbeam moved closer and closer to her, and then it went away... It was like Dad was opening his arms so she would not be so afraid of death.

~ Three sisters reflecting on the death of their mom

Additional Resources for Religious and Spiritual Guidance

Through the journey and at the end of people's lives, clergy and hospital chaplains are invaluable resources. They can:

- Visit homes, hospices, or hospitals;
- Administer sacraments or other religious rituals;
- Help individuals discuss their feelings and beliefs about death and their belief in God;
- Offer grief counseling and support;
- Provide resource information about community religious services;
- Help families plan funeral or memorial services.

Many times, along with social workers and bereavement and support services personnel, chaplains and clergy can connect patients and caregivers and facilitate volunteer efforts within a congregation to:

- Provide transportation, respite, meals, errands, household tasks, and yard work;
- Provide emotional and social support, including phone calls, visits, and check-ins;
- Give spiritual support, such as prayer, communion, spiritual conversation, and fellowship;
- Help with quality of life support, including transportation to social outings, gardening, help with hobbies, computer access, and art projects;
- Provide advocacy and resource support, such as finding community resources, helping with problem solving, and accompanying patients to appointments.

A CAREGIVER'S REFLECTION...

I work with many family members in the hospital. Because I see so many who are unrealistic, the last time I was with my dad, I said, "When you know, you tell me, and I will support it. I'm not going to like it, but I'm going to support it."

After a few days when I visited him, he told me, "We have to talk. This last month I've been sliding down hill." I asked him, "Do you think you're going to get better, Dad?" And he said, "No. It's going one way." So there it was laid out right in front of me. But he knew.

Later that day I talked with him about having some help. I told him we were going to contact the hospice people. I said, "Home care is so you can get better. Hospice care is to help us in the situation we are in right now." So he agreed that it was okay to have hospice come in.

Not every person can do this. You have to recognize the strengths that you have... that's where I just so believe that I was "sent" to those nursing homes to be trained so I could care for my dad. And I could do it...it was not a problem for me to take care of him.

Dad knew exactly what was happening. But Dad was okay with it... He had such a strong sense of family, friends, faith, and fun in his life. He was always very strong in his faith.

...When things changed, I could tell he did not have long. Before my "shift" was up, I told him how much all of us loved him, how much we were going to miss him, but that we were going to be okay with him gone. We would take care of each other...continue his legacy of taking care of each of us.

I know there is a beginning and end to this earthly life. I knew Dad's wishes. I thought it was important that you "release" [people who know they are dying], let them know that it is okay.

Later he took two final breaths and that was it. My dad had ninety-two years. In the end, how do you not celebrate that? It was like he scripted that.

~ Mary

LOL :)

While working for an organization that delivers lunches to elderly shut-ins, I used to take my four-year-old daughter on my afternoon rounds.

She was unfailingly intrigued by the various appliances of old age, particularly the canes, walkers, and wheelchairs.

One day, I found her staring at a pair of false teeth soaking in a glass.

As I braced myself for the inevitable barrage of questions, she merely turned and whispered, "The Tooth Fairy will never believe this!"

The Cycle of Life

Holidays are typically a time of joy and happiness. But while everyone else is immersed in the hustle and bustle of the season, there are many caregivers who are struggling with the holiday spirit while watching their loved ones succumb to illness or even death. I remember the first holiday season after my mom's stroke. Her weakened condition made it difficult for her to participate in all of the activities that were so much a part of our family's traditions. She had always made the pumpkin pies and baked her special nut bread. She had never missed a year of sending Christmas cards, some to people she had known for over sixty years. She prided herself on carefully selecting presents for each family member as well as her friends. My mom was a giver and it was important to her to keep giving.

My mom's persistence would not allow her to admit she could no longer perform these once simple tasks. It is difficult for someone who is no longer able to physically and mentally do the things he or she has spent a lifetime doing. The anger and emotions that played out during these months added increased stress to all of us involved in my mother's caregiving. We felt sad for her, sad for the loss of the traditions, and a bit less enthused about our own holiday festivities. But knowing it could be her last, we wanted to make it as good as we could. We helped her write and send cards, took her shopping, and wrapped the presents, but it just wasn't the same for her; she missed doing it herself. There was such a range of emotions to deal with along with all the other anticipated stresses during this trying time. Visits to my mom were difficult the weeks before and during this first holiday season. She missed her condo and would beg anyone who would listen to find a way to help her return home. We tried to decorate her room and make it feel festive, but nothing we did could even come close to matching the memories of holidays past in her own home. Understandably, she just simply lost the joy of the season.

My mom lived another eighteen months through anniversaries, birthdays, and additional holidays. We met the challenges of each day as best we could, again knowing in our hearts that it could be her last. I am glad we had all of those extra celebrations with my mom even if she was not fully able to enjoy them.

The passing of time allows the "not so good" times to fade and helps us clearly remember the "good" ones. Today when I think of the holidays, I picture my mom in the kitchen of my childhood home, hot pad in hand, carefully removing that pumpkin pie from the oven. If I concentrate hard enough, I can almost smell the freshly baked nut bread. I see colorful packages piled high under a towering, slightly crooked tree, in front of the bay window of our living room. Those are the memories that I want to keep.

Even though we lost my mom this past year, we added a new family member. I asked my new daughter-in-law the other day if she wanted to help me make nut bread! And so we pass the torches of yesterday as we make new memories and traditions. That is the cycle of life.

bottom photo circa 1943

Not everything that is faced can be changed. But nothing can be changed until it is faced.

–James Baldwin

The Empty Chair

Here are some excellent ideas for coping not only during the holidays, but on other special days: anniversaries and birthdays as well. Bittersweet may be the best word to describe what you are feeling. You feel the sweetness of the holidays, but the bitterness of your loved one's absence. Put together, they can give you a rich feeling of love for those present and for those gone whom you will never forget.

One of the most painful issues to deal with is how to survive the holidays after the death of a loved one. Because holidays are supposed to be family times, and because of the extraordinary (although unrealistic) expectations that you should feel close to everyone, this time of year can underscore the absence of your deceased loved one more than any other time.The important thing to remember is that you and your family do have options about how to cope with the holidays.These are a few things to keep in mind:

- As much as you would like to skip the entire holiday season, this is impossible.Therefore, it will be wise for you to take control of the situation by facing it squarely and planning for what you do and do not want to do to get through this time.
- Realize that the anticipation of pain at the holidays is always worse than the actual day.
- Recognize that what you decide for this year can be changed next year; you can move to something new or back to the old way. Decide what is right for you and your family now. Don't worry about all the other holidays to come in the years ahead.You will be at different places in your mourning and in your life then.
- Ask yourself and your loved ones to decide what is important for you to make your holidays meaningful and bearable.Then, through compromise and negotiation, see if everyone can get a little of what he or she wants and needs. Give-and-take is important here.

- Recognize that the holidays are filled with unrealistic expectations for intimacy, closeness, relaxation, and joy for all people — not just for the bereaved. Try not to buy into this for yourself — you already have enough to contend with.
- Be aware of the pressures, demands, depression, increased alcohol intake, and fatigue that come with holidays. As a bereaved person, you may feel these more than others. Take time out to take care of yourself during this time. You will need it even more.
- Re-evaluate family traditions. Ask yourself and your surviving loved ones whether you need to carry them on this year or whether you should begin to develop some new ones. Perhaps you can alter your traditions slightly so that you can still have them to a certain extent, but don't have to highlight your loved one's absence more than it already is. For example, you may want to have Thanksgiving dinner at your children's house instead of yours. Or you might open presents on Christmas Eve instead of Christmas morning.
- Do something for someone else. Although you may feel deprived because of the loss of your loved one, reaching out to another can bring you some measure of fulfillment. For example, give a donation in your loved one's name. Invite a guest to share in your festivities. Give food to a needy family for Thanksgiving dinner.

– The above is an excerpt from "Handling the Holidays," from *How to Go on Living When Someone You Love Dies,* by Therese Rando, PhD.

> "Compassion is to stand with someone through their pain."
>
> – Henri Nouwen

Anger, Fear, and Grief Revisited

My Grief is Different Now...

The anger that I felt for my mother at the beginning of her ordeal quelled over the ensuing months and transformed itself into compassion. I mellowed, accepting the inevitable and prayed that her suffering would be minimal and short-lived. Any fear that I experienced for her or for myself merely strengthened my own spirituality. I found myself having long talks with God about where my life was going, for I felt a newfound vulnerability over those things I could not control.

During the days and months after my mom's death, I concentrated on the plans for my son's October wedding. The event was bittersweet. My mom had so wanted to be there, but I think she might have known her chances were slim, for very early in the planning, she made sure that the flowers were her gift to Bret and Lauren.

My grief eventually took on the form of loneliness. Even though I lead a very active, busy life, I had to find a way to fill all of those moments and hours that I had spent with my mom. I would often find myself routinely picking up the phone to call her, or planning my day around my visits to her, only to realize that I was now the family matriarch, and could no longer turn to my mother or father for advice. I just didn't quite feel "wise" enough to be cast in that role.

It has been over a year since my mom's passing. I see her around me in the flowering forsythia bush she gave me. I think of her when I see a cardinal perched in a tree. When I look at the fliers for the spring clothing sales…I remember how she loved to shop. We made it through the first Thanksgiving, that first Christmas, and a first Easter without her. My grief is different now; it's peppered with a feeling of peacefulness and a heart full of memories.

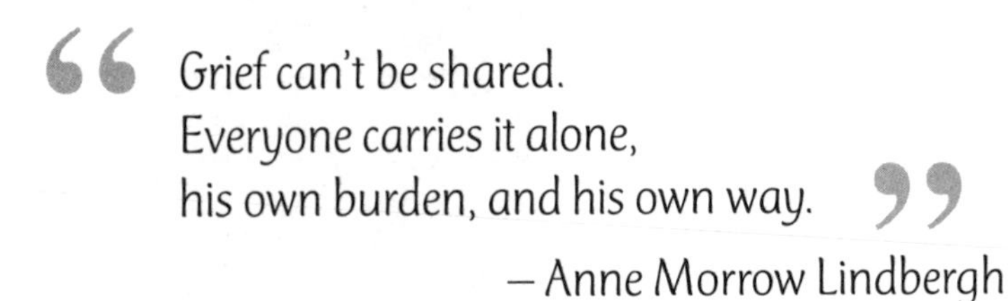

In his work, *Tasks of Mourning,* William J. Worden, Ph.D., identifies "tasks" that need to be confronted during the grief process. He stresses that a return to normal functioning and growth will bring about creation of new meaning in life. Among these are:

- Accept the reality of loss. The shock of the loved one's death slowly evolves into reality of what has happened. There is a need to really face the truth that the loved one is gone from our lives.
- Work through the pain and grief. When a loved one dies, there is "unfinished" business, guilt that we could have done more, regret that there wasn't as much time. Working through this can give one a sense of "purpose within our new life."
- Adjust to a life without the loved one. This involves performing the day-to-day jobs that may have been the responsibility of the deceased. For instance, the grieving husband may need to learn to cook or do laundry if that was always his wife's job.
- Emotionally relocate the deceased and move on with our new life. Our loved one will always be truly missed and longed for, but one can invest that energy into other relationships.

Moving Forward

A lot of people find comfort and relief by participating in a grief education or support group after a loved one dies. Many churches, hospital groups, and social service agencies offer programs for the bereaved. A formal support group may be beneficial to a particular individual while another may find reassurance and understanding in an informal get-together without agency sponsorship. Some people find it comforting to simply be with others who understand the loss they are experiencing, perhaps sharing coffee or lunch. You may need to explore a few different avenues before you find something that "fits" your comfort level.

The first year of loss is usually a very intense time of mourning. The following, from the Mayo Clinic at http://www.mayoclinic.com, provides some insight into the process of grief. Keep in mind that there is no timeline for grief.

Common Triggers of Grief — a Year of "Firsts"

Some reminders of your loved one are almost inevitable, especially during the first year after a death. That's when you will face a lot of "firsts" — those first special days that will pass without your loved one. As the weeks and months go by, you may also face other significant days or celebrations without your loved one that can trigger your grief again. Some of these "firsts" and other special occasions that can reawaken your grief include:

- The first holiday;
- Mother's Day, Father's Day, or another day you would have honored your loved one;
- Weddings and wedding anniversaries;
- Family reunions;
- Childhood milestones, such as the first day of school, prom, homecoming, and other child-oriented days;
- Anniversaries of special days — when you met, when you became engaged, when you last saw your loved one alive, when you took a big trip together.

Your reaction to these firsts and special occasions might be intense initially. But as the years pass, you'll probably find it easier to cope — but not forget. Reminders can be anywhere, and unexpected reminders aren't just tied to the calendar. They can be anywhere — in sights, sounds and smells, in the news, or on television programs. And they can ambush you, suddenly flooding you with emotions when you drive by the restaurant your wife loved or when you hear a song your son liked so much. Another death, even that of a stranger, can leave you reliving your own grief.

Even years after a loss, you may continue to feel sadness and pain when you're confronted with such reminders. Although some people may tell you that grieving should last a year or less, grieve at your own pace — not on someone else's expected timeline.

A CAREGIVER'S REFLECTION…

When I was in my early twenties, my mom died suddenly. Coming from a German-Irish family, grief was internalized and seldom expressed. Men were to be stoic. Yet it was the first time I had one of the significant people in my life taken from me.

As the months passed, we went on with life. I was training as a counselor and one of my experiences led me to have the privilege of "gowning up," watching a surgery first-hand. My mother had often told me of her love of medicine born of being a nurse in World War II. Observing the surgery, I suddenly understood my mom's enthusiasm. In the excitement of the day, I raced home to call her. When my parents' phone rang and rang and rang, I abruptly recalled that my father was working out of town that week and then, quite suddenly, I remembered that Mom had been dead for six months. My excitement had just overridden all the memories of her loss, and I realized how present she was still in my life. And would always be.

The years have gone by and she has had thirteen grandchildren; not one of them did she meet. Yet, I think all of them reflect who she was in the lives of her children. I have come to believe that love is stronger than death, and it does transcend our mortality.

~ Bill

> “You have known the blessing of sharing time with another, one whom you have loved deeply.
>
> You have been enriched by their life and have felt diminished by their death.
>
> You have lived it all:
> the laughter and the tears,
> the singing and the sighing,
> the darkness and the light.
> You have felt lonely and alone.
>
> Like so many others, you have been acquainted with grief.
>
> Like so many others, you have been taught the mysterious lessons of mourning.”
>
> – Anonymous

End Epitaph

As a result of this project, I have a greater appreciation for the wisdom of those around me, both young and old, and for the history they have created. I have an increased sensitivity to sunrises and sunsets, for the wonder of hummingbirds, for the beauty of spring flowers, and the miracle of newborn babies. I am less critical of those who have chosen different paths and far less concerned with images and expectations.

One of the only things we cannot dispute is that death is imminent for all of us. It is the when, where, and how that alludes us. Writing this book has been a cathartic journey that has allowed me to look introspectively at my life's triumphs and mistakes as a daughter, a mother, and finally as an aging adult in my own right. It has caused me to look in the mirror at my own mortality and shout back… "I'm not ready for this!!" As Kenny Chesney sings in "Lucky Old Sun,"

**"Everyone wants to go to heaven…
but nobody wants to go now!!"**

“To everything there is a season,
A time for every purpose under the sun.

A time to be born and a time to die;
A time to plant and a time to pluck up
that which is planted;
A time to kill and a time to heal...

A time to weep and a time to laugh;
A time to mourn and a time to dance...

A time to embrace and a time to refrain
from embracing;
A time to lose and a time to seek;
A time to rend and a time to sew;
A time to keep silent and a time to speak;
A time to love and a time to hate;
A time for war and a time for peace.”

– Ecclesiastes 3:1-8

Helpful Material

LOL :)

A young man saw an elderly couple sitting down to lunch at McDonald's. He noticed that they had ordered one meal and an extra drink cup. As he watched, the gentleman carefully divided the hamburger in half, then counted out the fries, one for him, one for her, until each had half of them. Then he poured half of the soft drink into the extra cup and set that in front of his wife. The old man then began to eat, and his wife sat watching, with her hands folded in her lap.

The young man decided to ask if they would allow him to purchase another meal for them so that they didn't have to split theirs.

The old gentleman said, "Oh, no. We've been married 50 years, and everything has always been and will always be shared, 50/50."

The young man then asked the wife if she was going to eat, and she replied, "It's his turn with the teeth."

Planning for the What Ifs

By James R. Tiedje, CSA

The hardest part of aging can be facing the reality that we may not always be able to handle everything on our own. In working with seniors on financial matters during my twenty-plus year career as a trust officer, I have seen the changes that often happen as aging occurs. Experience tells me that those who do their best to plan for the "what ifs" tend to be better prepared and reduce the risk that their financial matters will get out of control.

While one spouse may oversee the day-to-day financial details, it is always important for couples to discuss financial matters with each other. Both partners should:

- Know exactly what their assets are, where they are, and how to access them.
- Understand how to establish one's own credit, in one's own name after the death of a spouse.
- Understand how to structure their finances to minimize unnecessary expenses, avoiding excess taxes, hidden fees, commissions, inflation, or unscrupulous advisors.
- Know how to sell their home for the best price, buy a car without being over charged, and obtain insurance, both

long-term care and other, which provides the right coverage at the lowest possible cost.

- Know how to develop a financial plan that will allow them to live comfortably for the remainder of their lives.

The best time to make plans for the future is when you are in full control. From a financial standpoint, many can simply put into place a durable power-of-attorney to allow for their spouse or other family member to take over if it should become necessary to do so. Having a child listed as an additional signer on your checking accounts can also be helpful in the event of short-term disability. These options tend to work better for those parents who have children they trust, who live close by, and can stand ready to step in if needed. It can be a much more difficult matter choosing one child over another or for those who do not have children living nearby.

If you don't have children, finding the right person to trust can be extremely difficult. Many may be better served by creating a revocable living trust in which they can serve initially as their own trustee, but the trust document names a family member or a corporate trustee, such as the trust department of a bank, to take over in the event of their own inability to act. It is important to have a plan in place that works for you. I suggest you discuss these matters with your family and your attorney to see what plan is right for you.

What if you do nothing in the way of planning? If a disability does occur that requires someone else to attend to your financial affairs, your children or other family members may find it very difficult to step in. They could seek legal assistance that might lead to an establishment of a Guardianship or Conservatorship through the court system. These arrangements can be somewhat more public, disruptive, and cumbersome. Often, at this point, matters are already out of control and the potential of someone taking advantage of you is much higher.

So talk things over with your loved ones when you are able to make the decisions that are right for you. Do not put off things until they become an overwhelming task. Do it when you are in control.

James R. Tiedje, CSA, has served as a trust officer for over 25 years. His career started at Davenport Bank and Trust Company (now Wells Fargo) in Davenport, Iowa, where he was Assistant Vice-President Trust and Business Development Officer. He moved to Quad City Bank and Trust in 1997 and currently manages the relationships of over 100 clients, primarily seniors.

Legal Documents

There are many different types of legal documents that can help you plan how your affairs will be handled in the future. Many of these documents have names that sound alike, so make sure you are getting the documents you want. Also, state laws do vary, so find out about the rules, requirements, and forms used in your state.

- Wills and trusts let you name the person you want your money and property to go to after you die.
- Advance directives let you make arrangements for your care if you become sick. There are two ways to do this:
  - A living will gives you a say in your health care if you are too sick to make your wishes known. In a living will, you can state what kind of care you do and do not want. This can make it easier for family members to make tough healthcare decisions for you.
  - A durable power of attorney for health care lets you name the person you want to make medical decisions for you if you can't make them yourself. Make sure the person you name is willing to make those decisions for you.

For legal matters, there are two ways to give someone you trust the power to act in your place:

- A durable power-of-attorney allows you to name someone to act on your behalf for any legal task. It stays in place if you become unable to make your own decisions.
- A general power-of-attorney also lets you give someone else the authority to act on your behalf, but this power will end if you are unable to make your own decisions.

Advance Planning for Seniors

By D. Jamieson Long, Jr., J.D.

At some time in the process of caring for aging relatives, questions arise: "What legal documents are in place? What documents are needed?" Execution of legal documents is only a part of the process of advance planning, so the question of, "What documents are needed?" ultimately translates to, "What advance planning is necessary?"

Seek the Assistance of a Specialist

Elder law attorneys are lawyers who specialize in meeting the legal needs of the elderly. Because the incidence of disability rises as people age, many elder law attorneys find it necessary to become specialists in disability law as well. It is relatively common for elder law attorneys to limit their practices to elder and disability law. Most, but not all, elder law attorneys spend a substantial portion of their practice time dealing with advance planning for their elderly and disabled clients. Always ask.

It is often wise to seek the services of a specialist in order to avoid the hidden pitfalls general practitioners might not catch. This is especially true in the field of elder law. The multiple systems of complex and conflicting rules with which elder law attorneys find themselves dealing on a regular basis are often overwhelming to lawyers who don't specialize in elder law.

What Advance Planning is Necessary?

The first step — and the most essential step — in advance planning is to lay a solid foundation on which to build the plan. All the sophisticated planning in the world won't work if it isn't supported by a good foundation. The necessary foundation for appropriate and effective advance planning is "incapacity planning" or "adaptability planning," sometimes called "disability planning."

Clients — and some attorneys — too often make the mistake of thinking that the primary focus of advance planning is "estate planning" or "legacy planning." For many people, the first question that comes to mind when discussing advance planning is whether Grandma has a will. Has she made plans to leave an estate — or legacy — after death?

Let's be clear. Wills and death planning are often important components of the advance planning process. The primary focus of advance planning should, instead, be planning for the balance of a person's life, for the period from now *until* the end of life. Planning for the period of time after a person's death should be strictly a *secondary* component of advance planning. For this reason, some prefer the term, "life planning" to "estate planning" or "legacy planning."

Why is Adaptability Planning So Important?

Let's take Ann as an example. Ann's contingency plan to ensure her bills are paid during any period in which she can't do it for herself is to make her daughter, Jean, a joint tenant on Ann's checking account. However, if Jean becomes disabled herself, Ann's contingency plan is no longer operative. Jean is unable to pay Ann's bills. Ann must then find someone else to name as a joint tenant on her account who can assist her with paying the bills. But if Ann is already incapacitated when Jean becomes disabled, Ann is incapable of naming someone else to take Jean's place. Ann is incapable of adapting her plans, and her advance planning fails as a result.

Just as our lives and circumstances change over time, so our life plans need to adapt to our life changes. That is why the essential foundation of advance planning is building in the ability of the planning to *adapt and change* along with the person's life changes. Without this built-in adaptability, the otherwise sophisticated advance planning may quickly become outdated and unworkable.

In Ann's case, so long as she has full capacity, she can make the necessary changes to adapt her planning as her life and circumstances change. Upon her becoming legally incapacitated, however, Ann can no longer adapt her plans by her own actions. Ann will either have to rely on a surrogate she chose ahead of time, or she will have to rely on court intervention to do so.

The Consequences of Inadequate Planning

Advance planning is like fire insurance. We don't always use it, but when we need it, we can't do without it. Some people fail to plan at all. Others find out — often too late — that their planning is inadequate and can't be adapted on their behalf by anyone but themselves. Such cases can only be remedied by resort to the probate courts.

Let's take Ann's example again. Jean predeceases Ann. Ann neglects to replace Jean in her contingency plan. Ann later becomes incapacitated and can't pay her own bills. Ann alone has the power and authority to access her accounts and pay her bills, but she is incapacitated and lacks the ability to do so. At such point, only the probate court has the legal authority and power to access Ann's accounts and arrange for payment of her ongoing expenses and bills.

Those who do not adequately plan for incapacity are, in effect, planning for a trip to court. The adverse consequences of unwanted court intervention are several. Primary among them are:

- Court proceedings are costly;
- Court proceedings are public with the potential for accompanying loss of privacy;
- The court assumes control of the incapacitated person's affairs instead of someone who knows the person and may better understand his or her values and wishes; and

LOL :)

One of our patients wasn't taking any chances. Prior to her operation, she taped notes to her body for the surgeon: "Take your time," "Don't cut yourself," "No need to rush," "Wash your hands..."

After surgery, as I helped the patient back into her bed, we discovered a new note taped to her, this one from her doctor: "Has anyone seen my wristwatch?"

- Court proceedings are more narrowly governed by probate rules which often restrict the range of choices and options available to manage the incapacitated person's life and finances.

Unwanted probate court involvement isn't the only major adverse consequence of inadequate planning. Another is the increased potential for financial exploitation and other abuse. This may lead to the intervention of Adult Protective Services, which, may in turn, lead to the intervention of courts other than the probate court — for instance, the criminal courts.

In the complex world in which we live, the old saying holds truer than ever:

"Failing to plan is planning to fail."

D. Jamieson Long, Jr., J.D., is President of Jamieson Long & Associates in Moline, Illinois. He is the owner of the care coordination and advocacy service, GoldenCare Solutions Unlimited, LLC.

Resources

You may want to talk with a lawyer about setting up a general power of attorney, durable power of attorney, joint account, trust, or advance directive. Be sure to ask about the fees before you make an appointment. You should be able to find a directory of local attorneys at your library or you can contact the local bar association for attorneys in your area. An informed family member may be able to help you manage some of these issues.

What exactly is an "important paper?"

The answer to this question may be different for every family. The following lists can help you decide what is important to you. Remember, this is a starting place. You may have other information to add. For example, if you have a pet, you will want to include the name and address of your vet.

Personal Records

- Full legal name;
- Social security number;
- Legal residence;
- Date and place of birth;
- Names and addresses of spouse and children;
- Location of birth and death certificates; certificates of marriage, divorce, citizenship; and adoption records;
- Employers and dates of employment;
- Education and military records;
- Names and contact numbers of religious affiliations;
- Memberships in groups and awards received;
- Names and contact numbers of close friends, relatives, attorney, and financial advisor;
- Names and contact numbers of doctors;
- Medications taken regularly;
- Location of living will;
- Funeral home of preference.

Financial Records

- Sources of income and assets (retirement funds, IRAs, 401(k)s, interest, etc.);
- Social security and Medicare information;
- Insurance information (life, health, long-term care, home, car) with policy numbers and agents' names and contact numbers;
- Names of your banks and account numbers (checking, savings, credit union);
- Investment income (stocks, bonds, property) and stockbrokers' names and contact numbers;
- Copy of your most recent income tax return;
- Location of your most up-to-date will with an original signature;
- Liabilities, including property tax — what is owed, to whom, when payments are due;
- Mortgages and debts — how and when paid;
- Location of original deed of trust for home and car title and registration;
- Credit and debit card names and numbers;
- Location of safe deposit box and key.

Remember Well

By David Deuth, CFSP

In every society and in every generation, mankind has always honored the instinctual need to memorialize the lives of others at their death. Since the beginning of time, the human spirit has found it necessary to acknowledge that a life has been lived... that one mattered in time...that one made a difference in the world...and that one will not be forgotten.

Helping people "remember well" has become my greatest professional passion. While ample material exists to write an entire book on funeral-related topics, I want to share just a few real-life stories that best illustrate some important life lessons I've learned through the years.

On the Value of Visitation

After receiving my mortuary science degree over twenty years ago, I managed a funeral home in suburban Minneapolis. I had not been there very long when I encountered something I have not forgotten.

A middle-aged, professional man died unexpectedly. As I met with his family to finalize the arrangements for his service, they informed me they wanted a visitation and memorial service and requested that the body be cremated immediately. I arranged the details as requested. A few days later, with the urn on display in the chapel, guests began arriving to pay their respects and to offer their support to the family.

Early in the evening, as I greeted the family's guests, a man of similar age walked in; dressed in a suit and tie, I expected he may have been a colleague of the man who had died. As he signed the guest register, he turned to make his way into the chapel. Advancing only a few paces, he froze in place briefly before retreating back to me. "Where is the body?!" he inquired rather impatiently.

"The family chose to have the body cremated," I replied. What happened next was something for which I was totally unprepared to hear.

"That man," he said, choking up a little bit and pointing toward the chapel, "was my best friend. I drove three hours to come and say good-bye. They've taken that away from me..."

Stunned in my inexperience, I grasped for something — anything — appropriate to say. Before I could even respond, he spun on his heels and left. *He didn't greet the family.* He was hurting, and he simply wanted to honor his own need to say good-bye to his friend in a meaningful way. In his mind, he had been short-changed.

Lessons Learned

Although intensely personal to a family, every death will affect countless others outside the family circle: work associates, church family, civic clubs, volunteer organizations, customers, students… Funerals are intended to honor the one who has died, of course. But in many ways, funerals are for the family and everyone else whose lives the loved one touched. I've learned it is really important to try to consider these community needs too when making plans for a meaningful memory experience that will allow others to say their good-byes as well.

On Pre-Arrangement

Several years ago, I visited with a gentleman about the need for some pre-planning for his mother; a couple of weeks after, we completed the arrangements. His mother died about a year and a half later.

"We're so glad we got this in place when we did," he said with noted relief after her funeral. "It was really a good decision." Suggesting that *he* might consider pre-planning, I could see the "ah-ha" moment look come over his face. "I never thought about pre-arranging for myself," he said, rather surprised.

A short time later, we completed his plans. Songs and scripture readings were selected. He knew what he wanted for a casket, burial vault, even the flowers. Initially he decided to wait for pre-payment. The important thing, I assured him, was that the information was on file to let his family know what was important to him about his funeral.

When a few weeks passed, he called to say he had decided to get things pre-paid after all. As a divorcee, he didn't want his teenage daughter to be troubled by having something so important left undone. He felt it was well worth the peace of mind to have everything completed. The next day, he stopped by, and we finished the paperwork and payment.

That was a Tuesday.

Friday afternoon, his sister called to tell me that he had been killed in a tragic accident.

Lessons Learned

It's never too early to think about pre-arrangement.

On the most difficult day in the life of his family, I knew exactly what he wanted.

As a result, his family was able to be together and support one another instead of having to focus on the details and plans and expenses, wondering what he might have wanted.

Every day is a gift.

David Deuth, CFSP, is the President of Weert's Funeral Home in Davenport, Iowa. He has worked in the funeral and mortuary business for over twenty years.

Bibliography

Abramson, Alexis. *The Caregiver's Survival Handbook: How to Care for Your Aging Parent Without Losing Yourself.* New York: Berkeley Publishing Group, 2004.

"Agencies and Organizations." National Family Care Association. http://www.thefamilycaregiver.org (accessed January 31, 2010).

"Agencies and Websites." National Health Council. http://www.nhcouncil.org (accessed January 31, 2010).

Berman, Claire. *Caring for Yourself While Caring for Your Aging Parents: How to Help, How to Survive.* 3rd ed. New York: Henry Holt and Company, LLC, 2005.

Bozarth, Alla Renee, PhD. *A Journey Through Grief.* Center City, MN: Hazelden Foundation, 1990.

"Brief History of Hospice Movement." Hospice of Michigan. http://www.hom.org/movement.asp (accessed January 24, 2010).

Bursack, Carol Bradley. "Caregivers Often Suffer Unfounded Guilt." http://www.HealthCentral.com (accessed July 13, 2009).

"Caregiving Statistics." National Family Caregivers Association. http://www.nfcacares.org (accessed November 12, 2009).

"Final Details: A Checklist." American Association for Retired Persons (AARP). http://www.AARP.org (accessed December 10, 2009).

Ginsburg, Genevieve Davis. *Widow to Widow: Thoughtful, Practical Ideas for Rebuilding Your Life.* Cambridge, MA: Fisher Books Group, revised 2004.

"A Guide for the Newly Widowed." American Association for Retired Persons (AARP). http://www.AARP.org (accessed November 11, 2009).

Henry, Stella Mora, RN. *The Eldercare Handbook: Difficult Choices, Compassionate Solutions.* New York: Harper Collins, 2006.

Hogan, Paul, and Lori Hogan. *Stages of Senior Care: Your Step-by-Step Guide to Making the Best Decisions.* New York: McGraw Hill, 2010.

"Hospice for End of Life Care." American Association for Retired Persons (AARP). http://www.AARP.org (accessed November 20, 2009).

James, George. "A Survival Course for the Sandwich Generation: Carol Abaya Learned the Hard Way." *The New York Times,* January 17, 1999.

Kane, E.E. "Laughter Benefits: The Three C's." http://www.Lifescript.com (accessed January 22, 2010).

Levang, Elizabeth, PhD. *When Men Grieve: Why Men Grieve Differently and How You Can Help.* Minneapolis, MN: Fairview Press, 1998.

Loverde, Joy. *The Complete Eldercare Planner.* 2nd ed. New York: Three Rivers Press, 2009.

Martin, Mark. "Are You Caught in the 'Sandwich Generation?'" *The Christian Broadcasting Network.* http://www.cbn.com/cbnnews/healthscience.org (accessed August 4, 2009).

McFadden, Susan H. *Working with Seniors: Health, Finances, and Social Issues.* Fortress Press, 2003.

Miller, James E. *Seasons of Grief and Healing: A Guide for Those Who Mourn.* Minneapolis, MN: Augsburg Fortress Publishers, 2000.

Morris, Virginia. *How to Care For Aging Parents.* New York: Workman Publishing Company, 2004.

Rando, Therese A., PhD. *How to Go On Living When Someone Dies.* New York: Bantam Books, 1991.

Sheehy, Gail. *Passages in Caregiving.* New York: G. Merritt Corporation, 2010.

Sondrup, Corey, D.C. "Laughter: The Forgotten Medicine." http://www.selfgrowth.com (accessed October 14, 2009).

"Understanding the Power of Attorney." American Association for Retired Persons (AARP). http://www.AARP.org (accessed December 10, 2009).

Womack, Dorothy. "Caregiver Guilt." *Today's Caregiver.* http://www.caregiver.com (accessed January 24, 2010).

Worden, J. William, PhD. "Tasks of Mourning." *Grief Counseling and Grief Therapy: A Handbook for the Mental Health Practitioner.* 4th ed. New York: Springer Publishing Company, LLC, 2009.

Working with Seniors: Health, Financial and Social Issues. Society of Certified Senior Advisors. 2009.

LOL :)

Two ninety year-old women, Rose and Barb, have been friends all of their lives. When it was clear that Rose was dying, Barb visited her every day.

One day, Barb said, "Rose, we both loved playing women's softball all our lives, and we played all through high school. Please do me one favor: when you get to heaven, somehow you must let me know if there's women's softball there."

Rose looked up at Barb from her death bed and said, "Barb, you've been my best friend for many years. If it's at all possible, I'll do this favor for you." Shortly after that, Rose passed on.

A few nights later, Barb was awakened from a sound sleep by a blinding flash of white light and a voice calling out to her, "Barb, Barb."

"Who is it?," asked Barb, sitting up suddenly. "Who is it?"

"Barb, it's me, Rose."

"You're not Rose. Rose just died."

"I'm telling you, it's me, Rose," insisted the voice.

"Rose! Where are you?"

"In heaven," replied Rose. "I have some really good news and a little bad news."

"Tell me the good news first," said Barb.

"The good news," Rose said, "is that there is softball in heaven. Better yet, all of our old buddies who died before us are here too. Better than that, we're all young again. Better still, it's always springtime and it never rains or snows. And best of all, we can play softball all we want and never get tired."

"That's fantastic," said Barb. "It's beyond my wildest dreams! So what's the bad news?"

"You're pitching Tuesday."

Additional Resources

The following is not meant to be an exhaustive list of on-line resources, but it should be a good start to further your research about caregiving. There are many, many websites that are available and will serve you well. The ones listed highlight what might be available in any given field of care. Know that when you are researching on-line, you need to be attentive to accurate information and sources.

The National Institute on Aging, National Institutes of Health, and the U.S. Department of Health and Human Services provide a myriad of information on federal and non-federal resources. The web sites have links to many other federal agencies and in a few cases links to private organizations. You are subject to that site's privacy policy when you leave the governmental site. Reference in the websites to any commercial products, process, service, manufacturer, or company does not constitute an endorsement or recommendation.

The ***Administration on Aging*** is the official federal agency dedicated to the delivery of supportive home and community-based services to older individuals and their caregivers. The website has a special section on family caregiving. They can be reached at 202-619-0724 or at http://www.aoa.gov.

AgingCare.com helps people caring for the elderly find support, resources, and information, as well as a place to connect with other caregivers. They have a comprehensive collection of articles, news, product information, and a team of elder care experts who answer many tough questions caregivers have about caring for their loved ones. Most importantly, they provide a community in which caregivers can connect with others in similar situations to share ideas and help each other through the tough times. They can be contacted at 239-594-3235 and at http://www.agingcare.com/.

The ***American Association for Retired Persons (AARP)*** provides information about caregiving, long-term care and aging, publications, audio-visual aids, and much more for caregivers. AARP can be reached at 601 E Street, NW, Washington, DC 20049, 800-424-3410, or www.aarp.org.

The ***American Bar Association*** can be contacted at 321 N. Clark Street, Chicago, IL 60654-7598, 800-285-2221, or www.abanet.org.

A program of the National Hospice and Palliative Care Organization, ***Caring Connections*** is a national consumer and community engagement initiative to improve care at the end of life. They can be reached at 800-658-8898, or www.caringinfo.org.

Improving the health, safety, and well-being of America, the ***Centers for Medicare***

and Medicaid Services can be reached at 7500 Security Blvd., Baltimore, MD 21244-1850, 800-633-4227, 866-226-1819 (TTY), or www.cms.hhs.gov. The official website for the ***Centers for Medicare and Medicaid Services (CMS)***, the agency responsible for Medicare prescriptions is http://www.medicare.gov. The number is 800-633-4227.

Eldercare Locator provides referrals to Area Agencies on Aging via zip code locations. Family caregivers can also find information about many eldercare issues and services available in local communities. They can be contacted at 800-677-1116 or at http://www.n4a.org or http://www.eldercare.gov.

Family Caregiver Alliance (FCA) is a public voice for caregivers that illuminates the daily challenges they face, offers the assistance they need and deserve and champions their cause through education, services, research, and advocacy. They can be reached at 800-445-8016 and at http://www.caregiver.org.

The U.S. Department of Health and Human Services wants to help people stay healthy. ***Healthfinder.gov*** features links to more than 6,000 government and non-profit health information resources on hundreds of health topics including personalized health tools such as health calculators, activity and menu planners, recipes, and on-line check-ups. In addition, the site offers tips for caregivers and health news. Information is provided in English and Spanish. The department can be reached at www.healthfinder.gov.

Helpguide.org is a nonprofit group that helps people understand, prevent, and resolve many of life's challenges. They provide resources on topics such as mental and emotional health, family and relationships, and healthy living. You can get more information through http://www.helpguide.org.

The ***Homecare Directory*** at http://www.homecaredirectory.com is a search engine for listings concerning home health care, home healthcare equipment, hospice information, etc.

The on-line consumer database that lists ***Hospices in North America and the United States*** can be reached at 800-868-5171 or accessed at http://hospicedirectory.org/.

An ***Elder Care Survival Guide,*** www.howtocare.com/home.htm, provides information on home safety, nutrition, things you should know, and a myriad of elder care information.

Long-Distance Caregiving is dedicated specifically to the long-distance caregiver. This site offers resources to help you create solutions, provides advice from other caregivers, supports you in the community, and provides guidance to senior-serving professionals who have walked together. They can be reached at http://www.longdistancecaregiving.com.

The ***Mayo Clinic*** has some excellent resources on grief. Their website can be reached at: http://www.mayoclinic.com. You can search under "grief" for more articles and beneficial information.

The ***National Clearinghouse for Long-Term Care Information*** provides information on planning and financing long-term care, including planning for end of life care and all major types of public and private financing to help cover long-term care costs. They can be accessed at http://www.longtermcare.gov.

The ***National Elder Law Foundation*** illustrates the need for specialized attorneys and experience as certified specialists in certain fields of law. They can be reached at 6336 N. Oracle Rd., Suite #326, #136, Tucson, AZ 85704, 520-881-1076, or at www.nelf.org.

The ***National Family Caregivers Association (NFCA)*** is a national nonprofit organization dedicated to empowering family caregivers to act on behalf of themselves and their loved ones, and to remove barriers to their health and well-being. NFCA concentrates its efforts in three primary areas: education, building community, and advocacy. They can be contacted at 800-896-3650 and at http://www.thefamilycaregiver.org.

You can sign up for regular e-mail alerts about new publications and other information from the ***National Institute on Aging*** by accessing www.nia.nih.gov/healthinformation. A senior-friendly website from them and the **National Library of Medicine** can be found at www.nihseniorhealth.gov. This has health information for older adults, and it has special features which make it simple to use. For example, you can click on a button to have the text read aloud or to make the type larger. Leading the federal effort on aging research, the ***National Institute on Aging Information Center*** can be reached at P.O. Box 8057 Gaithersburg, MD 20898-8057, 800-222-2225, 800-222-4225 (TTY), or at www.nia.nih.gov, and www.nia.nih.gov/Espanol.

Some other helpful contacts are:
Alzheimer's Association, 800-272-3900, http://www.alz.org.

American Cancer Society, 800-ACS-2345, http://www.cancer.org.

American Diabetes Association, 800-342-2383, http://www.diabetes.org.

American Heart Association, 800-242-8721 (800-AHA-USA1), http://www.americanheart.org.

American Stroke Association, 888-478-7653 (888-4-STROKE), http://www.strokeassociation.org.

Mary Roberts
1920 - 2009

DAVENPORT — Mary Roberts, 88, of Davenport, formerly of St. Louis, Missouri, died Thursday, April 9, 2009, at Genesis Medical Center – West Campus in Davenport.

Mary was born in Macon, Georgia, in 1920, a daughter of Luther B. and Gussie (Moore) Jones. During World War II, Mary worked for McDonnell Douglas. On December 2, 1944, she was united in marriage to William "Bud" Roberts at Home Heights Presbyterian Church in St. Louis. Together, the couple owned and operated Roberts Buffet and Colonial Pancake House in St. Louis for many years. She later worked for Monsanto in St. Louis until her retirement. Mr. Roberts preceded her in death in 2002.

Following his death, she moved to Davenport to be near her daughter, Mary Schricker. While living in Davenport, Mary was very involved in many activities at CASI (Center for Active Seniors, Inc.) in Davenport and was a member of Newcomb Presbyterian Church. During her short time in the Quad Cities, Mary made many special and lasting friendships.

Survivors include her daughters, Brenda Lass-Stark (Rick), of Galena, Illinois, and Mary Schricker, Davenport; grandsons, Jason (Tami) Rudolph, San Diego, California, Matt Schricker, of Walcott, Iowa, and Bret Schricker and his fiancée, Lauren Nagle, of Buffalo, Iowa; one great-grandson, Trey Rudolph; two sisters, Thelma Bornefeld, of St. Louis, Missouri, and Dorothy Grohe, of Largo, Florida; and several special nieces and nephews.

In addition to her husband, Mary was preceded in death by her parents, sisters Myrtle Jones and Margaret Rookstolle, and brothers Luther B. Jones Jr., and Thomas Jones.

Mary Schricker

Mary Schricker earned her undergraduate degree in Speech and English at Northeast Missouri State, followed by a Masters Degree in Learning Disabilities from Marycrest University. She spent twenty-seven years teaching junior and senior high school special education, speech, and English. A member of the Local, State, and National Association of Realtors, Ms. Schricker is a practicing realtor in both Iowa and Illinois.

Ms. Schricker has written extensively on issues regarding senior citizens. She is a Seniors Real Estate Specialist (SRES) and a Certified Senior Advisor (CSA). She is actively involved in the Quad-City community, serving on the Board of Directors for Center for Active Seniors (CASI) in Davenport, Iowa, the Board of Directors and Executive Board of Directors for Friendship Manor in Rock Island, Illinois, as well as a founding member of SR Alliance.

Although born and raised in St. Louis, Missouri, Ms. Schricker moved to Davenport, Iowa, in the mid-1970s where she put down roots, made new friends, and raised her two sons. When she is not writing or spending time with family and friends, you will probably find her traveling, tending to her flowers, or curled up in a chair reading one of her favorite books.

Ms. Schricker is the published author of the biography, *The West End Kid: The Life of Dr. Jack Sunderbruch.*